The
Need
for a
New
Revival

The Holy Word for Morning Revival

Witness Lee

Frank Chen

Living Stream Ministry
Anaheim, CA • www.lsm.org

First Edition, June 2015.

ISBN 978-0-7363-7508-5

Published by

Living Stream Ministry
2431 W. La Palma Ave., Anaheim, CA 92801 U.S.A.
P. O. Box 2121, Anaheim, CA 92814 U.S.A.

Printed in the United States of America

15 16 17 / 4 3 2 1

2015 Memorial Day Weekend Conference

THE NEED FOR A NEW REVIVAL

Contents

Preface

1. This book is intended as an aid to believers in developing a daily time of morning revival with the Lord in His word. At the same time, it provides a limited review of the Memorial Day weekend conference held in St. Louis, Missouri, May 22-25, 2015. The general subject of the conference was "The Need for a New Revival." Through intimate contact with the Lord in His word, the believers can be constituted with life and truth and thereby equipped to prophesy in the meetings of the church unto the building up of the Body of Christ.

2. The book is divided into weeks. One conference message is covered per week. Each week presents first the message outline, followed by six daily portions, a hymn, and then some space for writing. The message outline has been divided into days, corresponding to the six daily portions. Each daily portion covers certain points and begins with a section entitled "Morning Nourishment." This section contains selected verses and a short reading that can provide rich spiritual nourishment through intimate fellowship with the Lord. The "Morning Nourishment" is followed by a section entitled "Today's Reading," a longer portion of ministry related to the day's main points. Each day's portion concludes with a short list of references for further reading and some space for the saints to make notes concerning their spiritual inspiration, enlightenment, and enjoyment to serve as a reminder of what they have received of the Lord that day.

3. The space provided at the end of each week is for composing a short prophecy. This prophecy can be composed by considering all of our daily notes, the "harvest" of our inspirations during the week, and preparing a main point with some sub-points to be spoken in the church meetings for the organic building up of the Body of Christ.

4. Following the last week in this volume, we have provided reading schedules for both the Old and New Testaments in the Recovery Version with footnotes. These schedules are arranged so that one can read through both the Old and

New Testaments of the Recovery Version with footnotes in two years.

5. As a practical aid to the saints' feeding on the Word throughout the day, we have provided verse cards at the end of the volume, which correspond to each day's Scripture reading. These may be cut out and carried along as a source of spiritual enlightenment and nourishment in the saints' daily lives.

6. The content of this book is taken primarily from the conference message outlines, the text and footnotes of the Recovery Version of the Bible, selections from the writings of Witness Lee and Watchman Nee, and *Hymns,* all of which are published by Living Stream Ministry.

7. The conference message outlines were compiled by Living Stream Ministry from the writings of Witness Lee and Watchman Nee. The outlines, footnotes, and cross-references in the Recovery Version of the Bible are by Witness Lee. Unless otherwise noted, the references cited in this publication are by Witness Lee.

8. For the sake of space, references to *The Collected Works of Watchman Nee* and *The Collected Works of Witness Lee* are abbreviated to *CWWN* and *CWWL,* respectively.

Memorial Day Weekend Conference

(May 22-25, 2015)

General Subject:

The Need for a New Revival

Banners:

God becoming man that man might become
God in life and in nature but not in the Godhead
is the essence of the entire Bible,
the "diamond" in the "box" of the Bible,
the eternal economy of God.

The high peak of the divine revelation is that
God became man so that man may become God
in life, nature, and expression
but not in the Godhead
to produce and build up the organic Body
of Christ consummating in the New Jerusalem
for the fulfillment of God's economy.

If we practice living the life of a God-man,
which is the reality of the Body of Christ,
spontaneously a corporate model
will be built up,
a model living in the economy of God;
this model will be the greatest revival
in the history of the church
to bring the Lord back.

In order to shepherd according to God,
we need to become one with God,
be constituted with God, live God, express God,
represent God, and minister God.

Reaching the Highest Peak
of the Divine Revelation
(1)
The Vision of the Age

Scripture Reading: Hab. 3:2a; Acts 26:19; Eph. 1:17; 3:9; Rev. 21:2

Day 1   I. Among God's elect there has always been an aspiration to be revived (Hab. 3:2a; Hosea 6:2; Hag. 2:7; Mal. 3:1; 4:2; Rom. 8:20-22).

Day 2   II. We can enter into a new revival by arriving at the highest peak of the divine revelation, the vision of the age, through the ministry of the age:

A. The particular recovery and work that God is doing in one age is the ministry of that age (cf. Gen. 6:16; 2 Kings 2:1-15).

B. In every age there is the vision of that age, and we have to serve God according to the vision of the age (Prov. 29:18; Acts 26:19; Eph. 1:17; 3:9).

C. God's word reveals to us that in every age He gives only one vision to man:

1. In order for us to serve God today, our vision must extend all the way from the first vision of Adam in Genesis to the ultimate vision of John in Revelation.

2. Today we can be in one accord because we have only one vision, an up-to-date, all-inheriting vision, the vision of the eternal economy of God (Job 10:12-13; cf. Eph. 3:9; 1 Tim. 1:3-4).

Day 3   III. In 2 Peter 1:12 *the present truth* can also be rendered "the up-to-date truth":

A. Although all the truths are in the Bible, through man's foolishness, unfaithfulness, negligence, and disobedience many truths were lost and hidden from man (cf. 2 Kings 22:8).

B. Freshly revealed truths are not God's new inven-

tions; rather, they are man's new discoveries;
every worker of the Lord should inquire before
God as to what the present truth is.

C. God's truths are cumulative; later truths do not
negate former ones; what we see today are the
cumulative revelations of God.

D. May God be gracious to us that we do not become the castaways of "the present truth"; may
we be watchful, and may we not allow the flesh
to come in or the self to gain any ground.

Day 4 IV. The highest peak of the divine revelation
given to us by God, the present truth, is the
revelation of the eternal economy of God:

A. The entire Bible, which is the explanation of the
eternal economy of God, is the autobiography of
the Triune God, seen in the two sections of eternity and on the bridge of time:

1. In the Old Testament there is the single,
but triune, God from eternity past, indi-
rectly moving only with men and among
men (John 1:1, 3).

2. He came from eternity into time and with
His divinity to enter into humanity to become the incarnated God for His direct move
in man, seen in the four Gospels, for the
accomplishment of His judicial redemption
(vv. 14, 29).

3. In resurrection He became the compounded
God, the all-inclusive life-giving Spirit, seen
in the Acts and the Epistles, for the carrying
out of His organic salvation (vv. 32, 42; 1 Cor.
15:45b; Phil. 1:19).

4. Because of the degradation of the church,
He became the intensified God, the sevenfold intensified life-giving Spirit, seen in
Revelation 1—20, for the producing of the
overcomers (1:4; 3:1; 4:5; 5:6).

5. In eternity future He will be the corporate
God, the New Jerusalem, seen in Revelation

21 and 22, for the universal, divine-human incorporation of the processed and consummated Triune God with the regenerated, transformed, and glorified believers as the goal of God's eternal economy (John 1:51; Rev. 21:3, 22).

6. Thus, the central revelation of God and the Lord's recovery is God becoming the flesh, the flesh becoming the life-giving Spirit, and the life-giving Spirit becoming the sevenfold intensified Spirit to build up the church that becomes the Body of Christ and that consummates the New Jerusalem.

Day 5

B. God becoming man that man might become God in life and in nature but not in the Godhead is the essence of the entire Bible, the "diamond" in the "box" of the Bible, the eternal economy of God (Gen. 1:26; John 12:24; Rom. 8:29):

1. God became man through incarnation by participating in man's humanity; man becomes God (in life and nature but not in the Godhead) through transformation by participating in God's divinity (John 1:14; 2 Cor. 3:18):

   a. Participating in God's life (John 3:15; 10:10; Col. 3:4; Rom. 8:10, 6, 11).

   b. Participating in God's nature (Eph. 1:4; 2 Pet. 1:4).

   c. Participating in God's mind (Eph. 4:23; Phil. 2:5).

   d. Participating in God's being (2 Cor. 3:18b; Eph. 3:8).

   e. Participating in God's image (2 Cor. 3:18a; Rom. 8:29).

   f. Participating in God's glory (v. 30; Heb. 2:10).

   g. Participating in God's sonship (Eph. 1:5; Rom. 8:23; Heb. 2:10-11).

   h. Participating in God's manifestation (Rom. 8:19).

Day 6

O i. To bear God's likeness (1 John 3:2).

j. To be Godkind—God's species (John 1:12; Rom. 8:14, 16).

2. This divine-human romance is the subject of the entire Bible, the content of God's economy, and the secret of the entire universe (S. S. 1:1; 6:13):

   a. Christ is divine and human, and His transformed lover is human and divine; they are the same in life and nature, perfectly matching each other.

   b. The Triune God, consummated to be the Husband, and the tripartite man, transformed to be the bride, are to be one couple, a corporate, great God-man (Rev. 21:2, 9).

3. God and man will become one entity, and that one entity is the mingling of divinity with humanity, which will consummate in the New Jerusalem, the conclusion of the entire Bible.

V. "I hope that the saints in all the churches throughout the earth, especially the co-workers and the elders, will see this revelation and then rise up to pray that God would give us a new revival—a revival which has never been recorded in history" (*Life-study of 1 and 2 Chronicles*, p. 15).

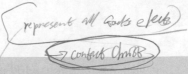
Morning Nourishment

Hab. 3:2 ...O Jehovah, revive Your work in the midst of the years...

Hosea 6:2 He will enliven us after two days; on the third day He will raise us up, and we will live in His presence.

[The] matter of revival is the "kernel" within the "shell" of the books of the Minor Prophets....Habakkuk 3:2a speaks of revival....Among God's elect there has always been an aspiration to be revived. As long as you are a saved one, every day, consciously or unconsciously, there is an aspiration with a spontaneous prayer within you: "O Lord, revive us." Although we may not realize it, such an aspiration has been within us through all the years of our Christian life.

God always considers His elect as a corporate Body. This means that Habakkuk and we are one in the unit of God's elect. Thus, when Habakkuk prayed for revival, we also prayed.... Such a prayer is an everlasting prayer. (*Life-study of the Minor Prophets*, p. 219)

Today's Reading

Without a revival, how could we have anything living? If we endeavor to practice just the first step of the God-ordained way—to visit people for the gospel—without being revived, this will be a heavy burden that no one can bear. We all need to realize that we have been saved and kept on earth to do one thing—to go to disciple the nations, beginning from "Jerusalem" and spreading to "Judea," to "Samaria," and to the uttermost part of the earth (Acts 1:8). If we live for our education, a career, a good marriage, or a nice house, that is vanity of vanities. We are living here for the spreading of the Lord Jesus, not merely to our neighborhood but to the entire world. If we would do this, we need to be revived. This is why the Lord has led us to practice the morning revival.

This matter of morning revival is according to the natural law in God's creation. God created the universe so that there is a sunrising every twenty-four hours. We believers should follow the sunrising to be revived every morning. Every day we need a "sunrising," and this sunrising is a revival. If we experience a daily revival, then we will be living and qualified to practice the God-ordained way and to help the church to take this way.

Hosea spoke of the desolation of the "two days" and the resurrection on the "third day": "He will enliven us after two days;/ On the third day He will raise us up" (6:2). Since to God a thousand years are as one day (2 Pet. 3:8), these "two days" may refer to a period of two thousand years. For almost two thousand years, from the time Titus destroyed Jerusalem and the temple in A.D. 70, Israel, our representative, has been desolate. From that year Israel lost the priesthood, the sacrifices, the prophets, the king, and the temple. Eventually, there will be the "third day"—the thousand years of the millennial kingdom— when Israel will be raised up, that is, restored.

The principle is the same in our Christian life. At a certain time we became desolate. After the two days of desolation, there is the third day, which signifies the pneumatic Christ in resurrection. Today we may receive the pneumatic Christ in resurrection and thus enjoy the reality of His resurrection. If we have the resurrected Christ, we are in the morning, the sunrising, and this is a real revival to us.

Joel 2:28 and 29 speak of the outpouring of the Spirit. Every day we need the outpouring of the all-inclusive, consummated, compound, life-giving Spirit as the processed and consummated Triune God. This all-inclusive Spirit includes Christ's divinity and humanity, the effectiveness of His death, and the power of His resurrection. This Spirit is our portion, our inheritance.

In the Minor Prophets there are both the divine Spirit, the consummated Spirit of God, and the human spirit, the stirred-up spirit of God's elect. The divine Spirit has been poured out, and our human spirit (the key to experiencing and enjoying Christ) responds to such a Spirit by being stirred up [Hag. 1:14a]. (*Life-study of the Minor Prophets,* pp. 219-221)

Further Reading: Life-study of the Minor Prophets, msg. 35

Enlightenment and inspiration: _____

_____ unconsciously _____

revive

Morning Nourishment

1 Sam. Then Jonathan the son of Saul rose up and went to
23:16-18 David at Horesh, and he strengthened his hand in
God. And he said to him, Do not be afraid, for the
hand of Saul my father will not find you; and you will
become king over Israel, and I will be second to you;
and even Saul my father knows that. And the two of
them made a covenant before Jehovah. And David
remained in Horesh, and Jonathan went to his house.

In the Old Testament both Solomon and David represented
the Lord. The two persons represented the one ministry in two
separate ways. In the Old Testament there were many ministries. After Moses, the judges were raised up. After that, there
was Solomon, the kings, and the prophets. After the Israelites
were taken into captivity, the vessels for the recovery were
raised up....In every age there is the ministry of that age. These
ministries of the ages are different from the local ministers.
Luther was a minister of his age. Darby was also a minister of
his age. In every age the Lord has special things that He wants
to accomplish. He has His own recoveries and His own works to
do. The particular recovery and work that He does in one age is
the ministry of that age. (*CWWN,* vol. 57, pp. 260-261)

Today's Reading

Jonathan stood between Saul and David. He was one man
standing between two ministries. He should have followed the
second ministry. However, because Jonathan's relationship
with the first ministry was too deep, he could not disentangle
himself. In order to catch up with the ministry of the age, there
is the need for us to see the vision.

It is God's mercy that a person can see and come into contact
with the ministry of that age. Yet it is altogether a different
thing for a man to take up the courage to forsake the past ministry. It is a precious thing to see, and it is a blessed thing to come
into contact with something. Yet whether or not one can set
aside his past ministry is entirely up to God's mercy. (*CWWN,*

vol. 57, "The Resumption of Watchman Nee's Ministry," p. 261)

We must be clear that in every age there is the vision of that age. We have to serve God according to the vision of the age. Consider the age of Noah. When we read...the Bible, it appears as if Noah's family, including himself, his wife, his three children, and their wives were the only ones who were serving God....Whether or not others were serving God, one thing is certain: They were not part of those who built the ark. For this very reason their service was not recognized by God.

The Bible shows clearly that in every age God gives only one vision to man. We cannot find in the Bible that there were two visions in any age. What about those men who came after the apostles' time? How did they serve God according to the proper vision? Today Paul is gone. If we are to serve God today, what is our vision?

During the past nineteen hundred years, countless numbers of Christians have been serving God....[Some] are serving according to the vision revealed in the New Testament Gospels, which has to do only with the earthly ministry of Jesus. Some serve without any vision at all. In order to serve God according to the up-to-date vision, we need to come up to the level of Paul's very last Epistles. In fact, we need to come up to the level of the epistles to the seven churches in Revelation as well as the revelation which covers all the ages, including the kingdom, the new heaven and new earth, and the ultimate consummation of the church—the New Jerusalem. Simply put, in order for us to serve God today, our vision must extend all the way from the first vision of Adam in Genesis to the ultimate vision of the manifestation of the church, the New Jerusalem. This and this alone is the complete vision.

Today we can be in one accord because we have only one vision and one view. We are all in this up-to-date, all-inheriting vision. (*The Vision of the Age,* pp. 13-14, 23, 48, 54)

Further Reading: CWWN, vol. 57, "The Resumption of Watchman Nee's Ministry," ch. 25; *The Vision of the Age,* chs. 1-3

Enlightenment and inspiration: _____

_____

_____

Morning Nourishment

2 Pet.   Therefore I will be ready always to remind you con-
1:12   cerning these things, even though you know *them*
     and have been established in the present truth.
2 Kings Then Hilkiah the high priest said to Shaphan the
22:8   scribe, I have found the book of the law in the house
     of Jehovah. And Hilkiah gave the book to Shaphan,
     and he read it.

The "present truth" [in 2 Peter 1:12] can also be rendered the "up-to-date truth." What is the up-to-date truth? Actually, all the truths are in the Bible; there is not one truth that is not in the Bible. Although they are all in the Bible, through man's foolishness, unfaithfulness, negligence, and disobedience many of the truths were lost and hidden from man. The truths were there, but man did not see them or touch them. Not until the fullness of time did God release certain truths during particular periods of time and cause them to be revealed once more. (*CWWN*, vol. 11, pp. 843-844)

Today's Reading

These freshly revealed truths are not God's new inventions. Rather, they are man's new discoveries. There is no need for invention, but there is the need for discovery. In past generations God revealed different truths. During certain periods of time, He caused men to discover these specific truths. We can see this clearly from the history of the church.

Take, for example, the raising up of Martin Luther in the sixteenth century. God opened his eyes to see the matter of justification by faith. He was a vessel raised up by God to unveil the truth of justification by faith. This does not mean that before Luther there was no such thing as justification by faith. The fact already existed before Luther's time. Luther was merely the one who realized this truth in a stronger way; he was particularly outstanding in this truth. For this reason, this truth became the "present truth" in that age.

Every worker of the Lord should inquire before God as to what the present truth is. We need to ask: "God, what is the present truth?" Although there are many major and crucial truths in the Bible, what we need to know is God's present truth. Not only do we need to know the general truths, we must also be clear about God's present truth.

We know that God's truths are cumulative; later truths do not negate earlier ones. All the past truths of God form the foundation of the truths today. What we see today are the cumulative revelations of God. When God opens our eyes to see this fact, we begin to realize that we are living in the tide of God's will. This tide is a continuation of all the past works of God in previous ages.

Our hearts are full of thanksgiving to God. From all these brothers we have received much help. As Paul said, "Neither did I receive it from man" (Gal. 1:12). In the same way, we can say that although we have received help from our brothers, these revelations were not received from man. We received help from Luther, Zinzendorf, the Moravian Brethren, and the Keswick messages. Today we believe that God's ultimate goal is to have Christ as everything. One elderly pastor, Dr. F. B. Meyer, also saw this matter....I believe that God has only one work today. It is the message of Colossians 1:18 which says that God desires to see Christ have the first place in all things. The basis of everything is the death, the resurrection, and the ascension of Christ. Other than Christ, there is no spiritual reality. This is God's "present truth."

We thank God that we can touch God's grand purpose. We need to humble and prostrate ourselves and to deny ourselves. We need to be clear that our work today is not just to save some souls or to help others become spiritual. Our goal is indeed the greatest and the most glorious. Thank God that we can know God's "present truth." May God be gracious to us so that we do not become the castaways of the "present truth." May we be watchful, and may we not allow the flesh to come in or the self to gain any ground. May God's will be accomplished in us. (*CWWN*, vol. 11, pp. 844, 856-859)

Further Reading: CWWN, vol. 11, "What Are We?" pp. 843-859

Enlightenment and inspiration: _____

_____

9. Nee's seeing was progressing --

_____

Morning Nourishment

John In the beginning was the Word, and the Word was
1:1 with God, and the Word was God.
Rev. ...Behold, the tabernacle of God is with men, and
21:3 He will tabernacle with them,...and God Himself
will be with them *and be* their God.

The Bible as the content of the Christian life is the autobiography of the Triune God....There is only one autobiography
which speaks of God, and this autobiography is the content of
the Christian life. (*The Christian Life*, p. 18)

John 1 reveals the two sections of eternity. How can God, who
had no humanity in eternity past, have humanity in eternity
future as His dwelling place?...Between these two sections of
eternity is the bridge of time. In eternity past God planned and
purposed, but He did not do anything. In eternity future God will
not do anything, because, at that time, everything will have been
accomplished. In eternity future He will simply enjoy His finished work....Everything that God needs to accomplish He ac-
complishes on the bridge of time. (*Life-study of John*, p. 58)

Today's Reading

The Bible with its sixty-six books opens with "In the beginning
God..." In the beginning of the Bible there was God only and nothing else. At that time God was only in His one aspect—the triune
Father, Son, and Spirit. Therefore, God referred to Himself as "Us"
and "Our." In Genesis 1:26 God said, "Let Us make man in Our image, according to Our likeness." This indicates that God is three—
the Father, Son, and Spirit—and therefore has the aspect of being
three. Besides this, there was nothing else. At the end of the Bible,
however, we reach the New Jerusalem. Between the beginning and
the end, there is a course of much history with many ages, including the age of the patriarchs, the age of the law of the children of Israel, and the age of the grace of the New Testament, in which many
things take place and in which God does a great deal of work. However, regardless of how many ages there are and how much work
God does, He has only one goal. In the beginning of the Bible there

is one single God, and at the end there is a great, corporate God—the New Jerusalem [John 1:51; Rev. 21:3, 22].

Just as the Bible begins with God, so it ends with God. In the beginning He is a simple God, a God who is triune; at the end a city appears, and that is the corporate God. The New Jerusalem is God's enlargement and expansion, God's expression in eternity, which is the corporate God. Those who participate in the New Jerusalem are all God's children, God's kind, God's species. (*How to Be a Co-worker and an Elder and How to Fulfill Their Obligations*, pp. 49-50)

We all need to have a clear view of the central revelation of God. The central revelation of God is God becoming flesh, the flesh becoming the life-giving Spirit, and the life-giving Spirit becoming intensified sevenfold to build up the church to issue in the Body of Christ and to consummate the New Jerusalem. We need to see that the Triune God became flesh, that the flesh became the life-giving Spirit, and that the life-giving Spirit became the sevenfold intensified Spirit. This Spirit is to build up the church, which becomes the Body of Christ consummating the New Jerusalem as the final goal of God's economy. This central revelation has been altogether neglected in today's theologies.

If we are asked to explain what the recovery is today, we should be able to answer in one simple sentence: The Lord's recovery is God becoming the flesh, the flesh becoming the life-giving Spirit, and the life-giving Spirit becoming the sevenfold intensified Spirit to build up the church that becomes the Body of Christ and that consummates the New Jerusalem. Regarding the Lord's present recovery, I hope that none of you would be held back by your old theology or by your old understanding of the recovery. (*The Divine and Mystical Realm*, pp. 17-18)

Further Reading: The Triune God's Revelation and His Move, msgs. 1-2; *The Move of God in Man*, ch. 1; *The Issue of Christ Being Glorified by the Father with the Divine Glory*, ch. 5; *The High Peak of the Vision and the Reality of the Body of Christ*, chs. 1-2

Enlightenment and inspiration: _____

_____

_____

Morning Nourishment

John 1:14 And the Word became flesh and tabernacled among us...

1 Cor. 15:45 ...The last Adam *became* a life-giving Spirit.

John 3:15 That everyone who believes into Him may have eternal life.

Many Christians care for the Bible as the "box," but they have not seen and do not appreciate the "diamond" which is the content of this box....The "diamond" in the "box" of the Bible is the revelation that in Christ God has become man in order that man might become God in life and in nature but not in the Godhead. (*Life-study of 1 Samuel,* p. 204)

Today's Reading

As God-men we have the divine right to participate in God's divinity. The phrase *participate in* means not only to partake of but to partake of for enjoyment. It indicates that we possess something and that we enjoy what we possess. We, the God-men, have the divine right to participate not in heaven but in God's divinity. We all need to realize that we can participate in God's divinity, that is, participate in God.

First, as the God-men we have the divine right to participate in God's life. John 3:15 tells us that everyone who believes in the Lord Jesus will have eternal life. Eternal life is the divine life, the life of God. We are human beings, but we can have God's life.

As God-men we also have the divine right to participate in God's nature....[In Ephesians 1:4] we see that God chose us in Christ with a particular purpose—to make us holy...even as He is holy (1 Pet. 1:15-16). To be holy is to participate in God's holy nature.

Because we have become God-men through regeneration, we also have the right to participate in God's mind. This means that we, who are human, can have a divine mind. Philippians 2:5 says, "Let this mind be in you, which was also in Christ Jesus." We need to let Christ's mind be our mind.

Next, the God-men have the divine right to participate in

God's being. Our basis for saying this is Paul's word in 2 Corinthians 3:18 about our being transformed into the Lord's image "even as from the Lord Spirit." This indicates that the work of transformation is done not by something of the Lord Spirit but by the Lord Spirit Himself. Hence, we are being transformed with God's very being.

Eventually, we will be brought into God's glory to participate in His glory. Hebrews 2:10 says that God is leading many sons into glory. Paul refers to this in Romans 8:30....Glorification is the step in God's complete salvation in which God will completely saturate our body with the glory of His life and nature. In this way He will transfigure our body, conforming it to the resurrected, glorious body of His Son (Phil. 3:21). This is the ultimate step in God's organic salvation, wherein God obtains a full expression.

As God-men we will participate also in God's manifestation (Rom. 8:19). When Christ our life is manifested, we will be manifested with Him in glory (Col. 3:4). Today God is hiding, but one day He will be manifested to the whole universe. Romans 8:19 indicates that when God is manifested, revealed,... [He] will be manifested with His sons, who will be the same as He in life, in nature, in mind, in being, in image, and in glory.

Finally, the God-men have the divine right to be Godkind—God's species (John 1:12; Rom. 8:14, 16). We have been regenerated to be Godkind. As God's sons we are God's kind, God's species.

[According to John 1:12] we have received the Lord Jesus by believing into Him, and God has given us the authority, the right, to be God's children. "The Spirit Himself witnesses with our spirit that we are children of God" (Rom. 8:16). Such a witnessing testifies to us and assures us that we are children of God, who possess His life....Wherever we may be we need to remember that we are God-men with the divine right to participate in God's divinity. (*Incarnation, Inclusion, and Intensification*, pp. 40-44)

Further Reading: Life-study of 1 Samuel, msg. 31; Incarnation, Inclusion, and Intensification, ch. 4

Enlightenment and inspiration:

participate — possess & enjoy

Morning Nourishment

S. S. *Come* with me from Lebanon, *my* bride; with me
4:8 from Lebanon come. Look from the top of Amana,
from the top of Senir and Hermon, from the lions'
dens, from the leopards' mountains.

Rev. And the Spirit and the bride say, Come! And let him
22:17 who hears say, Come! And let him who is thirsty
come; let him who wills take the water of life freely.

[In Song of Songs 4:8] Christ asks His lover as His bride to look
with Him from His ascension (Lebanon), the highest place of the
truth (Amana) and of Christ's victory in His fighting (Senir and
Hermon), and from the heavenly places of the enemies (the lions'
dens and the leopards' mountains). Christ calls His lover to live
with Him in His ascension, as He had called her to remain in His
cross (2:14)....She and Christ are living in one condition, the condition of ascension, to be a couple. Christ is divine and human, and His
transformed lover is human and divine. They are the same in life
and nature, perfectly matching one another. (S. S. 4:8, footnote 1)

Today's Reading

A human without a divine source cannot be the counterpart
of the God-man. Therefore, God regenerated His human elect.
Regeneration is to put divinity into humanity, to uplift humanity to the standard of divinity. However, regeneration does not
complete the process. We were regenerated in our spirit, but we
are not only a spirit. We are even more a soul. In order to uplift
our entire being, God first has to regenerate our spirit and then
transform our soul. The transformation of our soul takes time.
(*Crystallization-study of Song of Songs,* p. 88)

In Revelation 1:10 the apostle John told us that he was in
spirit—the mingled spirit—on the Lord's Day. This means that
John was a person who continually lived and walked in the
mingled spirit. Then, at the end of Revelation, as a closing of
the entire Bible, the Spirit and the bride speak together (22:17).
The bride is the church (2 Cor. 11:2; Eph. 5:31-32), and the
Spirit is the Triune God consummated to be *the* Spirit. This

Spirit is the Husband to the church. This indicates that the consummated Triune God will marry the transformed tripartite church. Thus, these two will become a couple—the Triune God consummated to be the Husband, and the tripartite man transformed to be the bride. The issue of such a union is the New Jerusalem [Rev. 21:2, 9]. (*Living a Life according to the High Peak of God's Revelation,* p. 24)

The holy city is a corporate person, and this corporate person is a couple—the processed Triune God married to the transformed, tripartite man. This is the Spirit and the bride becoming one (Rev. 22:17a). Divinity and humanity are married together, mingled together, to be one entity. The holy city is a corporate person—a corporate, great God-man. The holy city as the tabernacle of God is for God to dwell in (21:2-3), and God and the Lamb as the temple are for us to dwell in. God is our temple, and we are His tabernacle. In the new heaven and new earth, the New Jerusalem will be a mutual dwelling place for both God and man for eternity. (*Living in and with the Divine Trinity,* pp. 134-135)

Christ made Himself, the first God-man, a prototype for the mass reproduction of many brothers—the many God-men (Rom. 8:29). I have been a Christian for about sixty-nine years. After so many years, I have been made by God to know only one thing—God became man so that man may become God in life and in nature but not in the Godhead. This is my unique burden, my unique message. God and man will become one entity, and that one entity is the mingling of divinity with humanity. This mingling will consummate in the New Jerusalem, which is the conclusion of the entire Bible. (*The Practical Way to Live a Life according to the High Peak of the Divine Revelation in the Holy Scriptures,* p. 27)

Further Reading: Crystallization-study of Song of Songs, msgs. 7, 9; *Living a Life according to the High Peak of God's Revelation,* ch. 3; *Living in and with the Divine Trinity,* ch. 13; *The Practical Way to Live a Life according to the High Peak of the Divine Revelation in the Holy Scriptures,* ch. 2

Enlightenment and inspiration: _____

_____

Lebanon— white mountain...

Change = by falling in (love) w our Lord .

What Miracle! What Mystery!

1   What miracle! What mystery!
That God and man should blended be!
God became man to make man God,
Untraceable economy!
From His good pleasure, heart's desire,
His highest goal attained will be.

2   Flesh He became, the first God-man,
His pleasure that I God may be:
In life and nature I'm God's kind,
Though Godhead's His exclusively.
His attributes my virtues are;
His glorious image shines through me.

3   No longer I alone that live,
But God together lives with me.
Built with the saints in the Triune God,
His universal house we'll be,
And His organic Body we
For His expression corp'rately.

4   Jerusalem, the ultimate,
Of visions the totality;
The Triune God, tripartite man—
A loving pair eternally—
As man yet God they coinhere,
A mutual dwelling place to be;
God's glory in humanity
Shines forth in splendor radiantly!

Composition for prophecy with main point and sub-points: _____

Vision of the age — present truth
— diamond in the box

**Reaching the Highest Peak
of the Divine Revelation
(2)
Becoming God in Life, Nature,
and Expression
to Produce the Body of Christ
Consummating in the New Jerusalem**

Scripture Reading: Eph. 3:9; John 1:1, 14; 12:24; Rom. 8:29;
2 Cor. 3:18; Rev. 21:2, 9-11

Day 1

I. **God's eternal economy is to make man the same as He is in life, nature, and expression but not in the Godhead and to make Himself one with man and man one with Him, thus to be enlarged and expanded in His expression, that all His divine attributes may be expressed in human virtues (Eph. 3:9; 1:10):**

A. The main contents of the New Testament are that the Triune God has an eternal economy according to His good pleasure to dispense Himself into His chosen and redeemed people in His life and nature to make them His duplication so that they may express Him; this corporate expression is the Body of Christ consummating in the New Jerusalem (3:9-21; Rev. 21:2, 9-11).

B. God's economy is His intention to dispense Himself in His Divine Trinity into His chosen and redeemed people to be their life and nature so that they may be the same as He is for His corporate expression (1 Tim. 1:4; Eph. 1:3-23).

C. God's good pleasure is to be one with man and to make man the same as He is in life, nature, and expression but not in the Godhead (vv. 5, 9).

Day 2

D. For the accomplishment of His economy, God created us in His own image with the intention that we would become God in life and nature but not in the Godhead (Gen. 1:26; Rev. 4:3; 21:10-11).

E. God became man in order to have a mass repro-

duction of Himself and thereby to produce a new
kind—God-man kind (John 1:1, 14; 12:24; Heb.
2:10):

1. God sent His Son to be a man and to live a
   God-man life by the divine life (John 3:16;
   1:14; 6:57).

Day 3

Korean

2. The God-man living issues in a universal, great
   man who is exactly the same as Christ—a corporate God-man who lives a God-man life by
   the divine life for the manifestation of God
   in the flesh (Eph. 4:24; 1 Tim. 3:15-16).

F. God's economy, as recorded in the Scriptures, is
   that God became man to make man God in life,
   nature, and expression so that we may have a
   God-man living and become the Body of Christ
   (Rom. 8:3; 1:3-4; 8:4, 14, 29; 12:4-5).

Day 4

Warners

II. **The high peak of the divine revelation is that
    God became man so that man may become
    God in life, nature, and expression but not in
    the Godhead to produce and build up the
    organic Body of Christ consummating in the
    New Jerusalem for the fulfillment of God's
    economy to close this age and bring Christ
    back to set up His kingdom (John 1:12-14;
    1 John 3:1-2; Rom. 8:3; 12:4-5; Rev. 11:15):**

A. God has a heart's desire and an eternal purpose;
   He wants to make Himself man and to make
   man God so that the two—God and man—may
   be the same in life, nature, and expression (Eph.
   1:5, 9; 3:11; 4:16; 5:30, 32).

B. God redeemed us for the purpose of making us
   God in life and nature so that He can have the
   Body of Christ, which consummates in the New
   Jerusalem as God's enlargement and expression
   for eternity (1:7; 4:16; Rev. 21:2).

C. The One who is God yet man dwells in the one
   who is man yet God, and the one who is man yet
   God dwells in the One who is God yet man; thus,

they are a mutual dwelling place (John 14:2-3, 20, 23; 15:4).

D. God became man to make man God in life, nature, and expression through a marvelous process:

　　1. With God this process was incarnation, human living, crucifixion, and resurrection (1:14; 6:57a; 1:29; 3:14; 12:24; 20:22).

　　2. With man this process is regeneration, sanctification, renewing, transformation, conformation, and glorification (3:6; Rom. 12:2).

　　3. In Paul's Epistles we see the ascended Christ ministering Himself to us as the life-giving Spirit to transform us into His image, making us the same as He is in life, nature, and expression (2 Cor. 3:17-18; Rom. 8:29).

Day 5

E. It is only by God's becoming man to make man God in life, nature, and expression that the Body of Christ can be produced and built up; this is the high peak of the divine revelation given to us by God (v. 3; 1:3-4; 8:14, 16, 29; 12:4-5):

　　1. The reality of the Body of Christ is a corporate living by a group of God's redeemed who have been made God, the God-men, by God and who live not by themselves but by another life, which is the processed and consummated Triune God (Gal. 2:20).

　　2. The highest peak in God's economy is the reality of the Body of Christ (Rom. 8:2, 6, 10-11; 12:4-5).

　　3. The reality of the Body of Christ is the union and mingling of God and man to live out a corporate God-man (John 14:20; 15:4; Eph. 4:4-6, 24).

Day 6

F. The New Jerusalem, the ultimate consummation of the Bible, involves God becoming man and man becoming God in life, nature, and expression but not in the Godhead (Rev. 21:2, 9-11; 3:12):

　　1. The New Jerusalem is a composition of

divinity and humanity mingled, blended, and
built up together as one entity (John 14:20,
23; Rev. 21:9-11):

a. All the components have the same life,
nature, and constitution and thus are a
corporate person.

b. God and man, man and God, are built up
together by being blended and mingled
together; this is a matter of God becoming man and man becoming God in life,
nature, and expression but not in the
Godhead (John 14:20, 23; 1 Cor. 6:17).

2. The New Jerusalem is a composition of
God's chosen, redeemed, regenerated, sanctified, renewed, transformed, conformed,
and glorified people who have been deified
(John 3:6; Heb. 2:11; Rom. 12:2; 8:29-30):

a. For us to be deified means that we are
being constituted with the processed and
consummated Triune God so that we may
be made God in life, nature, and expression to be His corporate expression for
eternity (Rev. 21:11).

b. The deification of the believers is a process that will consummate in the New
Jerusalem; this is the highest truth and
the highest gospel (3:12).

Morning Nourishment

Eph. And to enlighten all *that they may see* what the econ-
3:9 omy of the mystery is, which throughout the ages
has been hidden in God, who created all things.
1:10 Unto the economy of the fullness of the times, to
head up all things in Christ, the things in the heavens and the things on the earth, in Him.

The Triune God has one heart's desire (Eph. 1:5, 9). According to His heart's desire, God made His eternal economy (1 Tim.
1:4b; Eph. 1:10; 3:9) to make man the same as He is in life and
nature but not in His Godhead and to make Himself one with
man and man one with Him, thus to be enlarged and expanded
in His expression, that all His divine attributes may be expressed in human virtues. (*The Ten Great Critical "Ones" for
the Building Up of the Body of Christ*, p. 14)

Today's Reading

The main contents of the New Testament are that the Triune
God has an eternal economy according to His good pleasure to dispense Himself into His chosen and redeemed people in His life and
in His nature, to make all of them the same as He is in life and nature, to make them His duplication that they may express Him.
This corporate expression will consummate in the New Jerusalem.
Thus, the New Jerusalem is simply the enlarged, the increased, incarnation consummated in full, that is, the fullness of the Triune
God for Him to express Himself in His divinity mingled with humanity. These are the contents of the New Testament.

The Bible, which consists of sixty-six books, begins with God
and His creation in Genesis and consummates with the New
Jerusalem in Revelation. Between these two ends of the Bible,
there are history, teachings, prophecies, and types. But if we
understand the Bible only according to these things, we still do
not know the Bible. We need to see the eternal economy of God,
which is God's eternal intention with His heart's desire to dispense Himself in His Divine Trinity as the Father in the Son by
the Spirit into His chosen people to be their life and nature that

they may be the same as He is for His fullness, His expression.

An economy is an arrangement to carry out a plan for dispensing. God's economy is God's plan, God's arrangement, for God to dispense Himself in His element, life, nature, and attributes, and all that He has achieved and attained into His chosen people that they may be rebuilt by being constituted with the divine essence in the divine element of the divine source to be something divine. Before receiving God's dispensing, we were merely human. After God's rebuilding with the divine constitution we, like the Lord Jesus, become divinely human and humanly divine. Before incarnation Christ was only divine, but after His incarnation He became a God-man, a man with the divine nature. Now He is divinely human, and He is also humanly divine. Having been regenerated by Christ, we have become a part of Him, and now we are the same as He is—divinely human and humanly divine. (*Life-study of Job*, pp. 64, 57-58)

Ephesians 1:5 says that God predestinated us unto sonship according to the good pleasure of His will. *Unto sonship* means to make us sons. God predestinated us, marked us out, before the foundation of the world that we could be made His sons according to His good pleasure.

Ephesians 1:9 also speaks of God's good pleasure, which He purposed in Himself. God has some plan to fulfill, and this plan is to have the church as the Body of Christ which consummates in the New Jerusalem. We need the entire Bible to understand this one verse of the Bible in Ephesians. The good pleasure of God is to have us as His sons, and eventually, all these sons ultimately consummate the New Jerusalem. We should not forget these items— first, God loves us and second, He has a good pleasure. According to the revelation of the Bible, God's good pleasure is to have many sons and have all these many sons consummated as the New Jerusalem. (*The God-man Living*, pp. 3-4)

Further Reading: The Governing and Controlling Vision in the Bible, ch. 1; Life-study of Job, msgs. 9-10

Enlightenment and inspiration: _____

_____

_____

_____

Morning Nourishment

Gen. And God said, Let Us make man in Our image, ac-
1:26 cording to Our likeness...

Heb. For it was fitting for Him, for whom are all things
2:10 and through whom are all things, in leading many
sons into glory, to make the Author of their salvation perfect through sufferings.

God created us for the accomplishment of His eternal economy
in His own image with the intention that we could become Him in
life and nature but not in the Godhead. For this purpose He created
us with a spirit to receive Him. Many people do not realize that God
also created us with a seeking heart for Himself so that He could be
our satisfaction. (*Crystallization-study of Song of Songs*, p. 9)

Today's Reading

Two thousand years after Abraham, the choosing God became
a man. This God-man, through His death and resurrection, has
made a mass reproduction of Himself. He as the one grain became
many grains (John 12:24). The many grains are ground into fine
flour and blended together to become one loaf (1 Cor. 10:17). The
Lord Jesus as the only begotten Son of God was the one grain, and
He made us the many grains, His many "twins," His many brothers (Rom. 8:29), to be blended into one loaf, one Body. Among us
there is no difference in nationality, race, or social rank (Col. 3:11).
We are a new kind, "God-man kind."

Just as there are new words to describe new developments in
human culture, so we need new terms and expressions to describe
matters in our spiritual culture. *God-man kind* is such an expression. In Christ God and man have become one entity, the God-man.
In God's creation there was no mankind; there was only man as
God's kind. It was through man's fall that mankind came into existence. Eventually God became a man to have a mass reproduction
of Himself and thereby to produce a new kind. This new kind is neither God's kind nor mankind—it is God-man kind. Today as believers in Christ, we are God-man kind; we are God-men.

Do you know what God wants today? We may say that He

wants Christians and believers in Christ. Actually, what God wants is not merely Christians or even believers in Christ; He wants a big group of God-men. I believe that our God, who is sitting in the heavens, is happy whenever He looks upon a gathering of God-men.

When we think of ourselves as God-men, this thinking, this realization, revolutionizes us in our daily experience. For example, a brother may be unhappy with his wife. But he remembers that he is a God-man, and immediately his attitude is changed. Then he will desire to be a God-man husband.

In God's view *mankind* is a negative term referring to fallen man. As believers in Christ and children of God, we are not mankind—we are God-man kind....When we realize that we are God-men, we will say, "Lord, You are the first God-man, and we are the many God-men following You. You lived a human life, not by Your human life but by God's divine life to express Him. His attributes became Your virtues. You were here on this earth dying every day. You were crucified to live. Lord, You are my life today and You are my person. You are just me. I therefore must die. I need to be conformed to Your death. I have to be crucified to die every day to live a God-man's life, a human life yet not by my human life but by the divine life, with Your life and Your nature as my constitution to express You in Your divine attributes, which become my human virtues." This makes us not just a Christian or a believer in Christ but a God-man, one kind with God. This is the highest point of God's gospel.

After hearing that God wants a group of God-men, how can you be content to be anything else? What do you want to be? Do you want to be a typical Chinese or a typical American? Do you want to be merely a Christian or a believer in Christ? We should all declare that we want to live the life of a God-man. Eventually, the God-men will be the victors, the overcomers, the Zion within Jerusalem. (*Life-study of 1 & 2 Chronicles,* pp. 24-25, 27-28)

Further Reading: Life-study of 1 & 2 Chronicles, msg. 4; *Crystallization-study of the Epistle to the Romans,* msg. 17

Enlightenment and inspiration: _____

_____

_____

_____

Morning Nourishment

Rom. Because those whom He foreknew, He also predesti-
8:29 nated *to be* conformed to the image of His Son, that
He might be the Firstborn among many brothers.
12:4-5 For just as in one body we have many members,
and all the members do not have the same function, so we who are many are one Body in Christ,
and individually members one of another.

The New Testament reveals to us a great, mysterious, and
universal man, with Jesus Christ as the Head and all the believers as the Body. The Gospels, the first four books of the New Testament, reveal to us Christ as the Head; then Acts reveals the
Body. In Acts we see Christ acting, living, moving, and working
in His Body. Some people refer to Acts as the acts of the apostles,
but strictly speaking, Acts is the acts of Christ as the Spirit
through the apostles, and not only through the apostles but also
through all the disciples, through all the believers, through the
whole Body. Hence, Acts is the acts of the Head as the Spirit
through the Body. Thus, we see the universal, great man—the
Head with the Body. (*CWWL, 1963,* vol. 2, "The Central Thought
of God," p. 394)

Today's Reading

Although we cannot find the term *the Triune God* in the Bible,
nearly all Bible students recognize that the entire Bible reveals
the Triune God. In the same principle, although we cannot find
the term *the God-men* in the Bible, the fact, the reality, of the God-
men is in the Bible. Initially, the Bible speaks of the God-man.
Today this God-man has become the God-men. The God-man is
Jesus Christ, who is God incarnated to be a man. As such a One,
He is the God-man. Furthermore, He is the model God-man, the
prototype for the producing of many God-men (Rom. 1:3-4; 8:29),
including all the dear saints throughout the world. Regardless of
our nationality, and regardless of whether we are male or female,
young or old, we all must believe that we are God-men. We are all
God-men, and each one of us is a God-man.

Eventually, the Bible builds up a corporate man. Ultimately, this corporate man will be enlarged to be its consummation, the New Jerusalem. The issue of the Bible's teaching is just one entity, the New Jerusalem as the aggregate of all the God-men.

This is for the manifestation of God in the flesh as the new man (1 Tim. 3:16; Eph. 2:15). First Timothy 3:16 says, "And confessedly, great is the mystery of godliness: He who was manifested in the flesh." According to the context of this verse, godliness here refers not only to piety but also to the living of God in the church, that is, to God as life lived out in the church. Godliness means that God becomes man and man becomes God. This is a great mystery in the universe. God has become man so that man may become God to produce a corporate God-man for the manifestation of God in the flesh as the new man.

This corporate God-man grows up for the purpose of building up the organic Body of Christ for the fulfillment of the eternal economy of God (Eph. 4:12-13, 15-16). The manifestation of God is possible by the Body of Christ. The Body of Christ is just the manifestation of God for the fulfillment of the eternal economy of God. Regardless of how much our natural self can be built up, and regardless of how much our natural capacity can be cultivated, we can never be the manifestation of God, and we can never be a part of the Body of Christ. This must be the responsibility of the God-men. The God-men are born of God to have God's life and God's nature, to live by a mingled life in a mingled nature, to build up the Body of Christ as God's manifestation. This is the revelation of the Bible. The natural concept we have received from human philosophy and religion is not the revelation of the Bible. The Bible does not teach this. The Bible teaches that a man must be born of God to be a God-man, and this God-man must be raised up, must grow up. Then the God-men know how to build up themselves to be the Body of Christ for the manifestation of God and for the fulfillment of God's economy. (*The God-men,* pp. 10, 14-15)

Further Reading: The God-men, ch. 1; *The God-man Living,* ch. 1

Enlightenment and inspiration: _____

_____

_____

_____

Morning Nourishment

John
1:14   And the Word became flesh and tabernacled among
us (and we beheld His glory, glory as of the only
Begotten from the Father), full of grace and reality.

12:24   Truly, truly, I say to you, Unless the grain of wheat
falls into the ground and dies, it abides alone; but if
it dies, it bears much fruit.

We definitely have a burden to focus on the unique, highest, deepest, most mysterious, and most glorious subject in the Holy Scriptures, that is, God's highest purpose concerning man....The Bible is a book concerning God, especially concerning God's relationship with man. In God's relationship with man we can see that God has a heart's desire and a purpose; that is, God wants to make Himself man and to make man God that the two—God and man—may become altogether the same. God is God, yet He made Himself a man and lived a human life exactly the same as man in the human nature and the human life....Man is man, yet God wants to make man the same as He is, of the same kind and the same likeness as He is in life and in nature, except that we human beings have no share in His person. Thus, His attributes become our human virtues and His glorious image is expressed and lived out through us. Eventually, God and man become a matching pair in the universe. (*The Dispensing, Transformation, and Building of the Processed Divine Trinity in the Believers*, p. 9)

Today's Reading

[God] is God, yet He took on human nature, put on a human body, and had a human life to dwell and live together with men in order to make men, His chosen people, the same as He is. Thus, although these men are human, they have His divine life and His divine nature. In life and nature, man and God are of the same kind. Eventually, He begot us, and we were born of Him. He is God and has our human nature; likewise, we are man and also have His divine nature. Hence, these two are God yet with humanity and are man yet with divinity. By these two natures and two lives God mingles Himself with man in order that His divine life may be lived out through humanity among men, and in order that His redeemed may have His divinity and in His divinity may live out the likeness of God through the resurrected and uplifted humanity.

Eventually, this will make God and man alike and mingled together and even built together....God builds Himself into man and builds man into Himself. He Himself becomes this constitution with Himself as the intrinsic element—the source, element, and essence within—and with His redeemed people built together in the intrinsic element—the source, element, and essence—to become the framework. This is the one new man in the universe.... The ultimate consummation of this new man is the New Jerusalem. The New Jerusalem is a constitution of God and man and man and God, who are constituted into one; it is divinity expressed in humanity and humanity glorified in divinity. Therefore, they two—divinity and humanity—become a mutual dwelling place. The One who is God yet man dwells in the one who is man yet God, and the one who is man yet God dwells in the One who is God yet man. They are a mutual dwelling place. Thus, His divine glory shines forth radiantly with great splendor in humanity. There is not one bit of good or evil here, and it has nothing to do with good and evil. God's economy is absolutely outside of good and evil. This economy is God and man becoming one entity, as one who is God yet man and man yet God. (*The Dispensing, Transformation, and Building of the Processed Divine Trinity in the Believers*, pp. 37-38)

In this economy God became man in order to make man God in life and nature (but not in the Godhead) through a marvelous process. With God this process was incarnation, human living, death, and resurrection. With us this process is regeneration, sanctification, renewing, transformation, conformation, and glorification. God has become man, and eventually man will become God in life and in nature. Then the eternal economy of God will be accomplished. (*Life-study of 1 & 2 Kings*, p. 145)

Further Reading: The Dispensing, Transformation, and Building of the Processed Divine Trinity in the Believers, chs. 1, 4

Enlightenment and inspiration: _____

_____

_____

_____

Morning Nourishment

Eph. **One Body and one Spirit, even as also you were**
4:4-6 **called in one hope of your calling; one Lord, one**
faith, one baptism; one God and Father of all, who
is over all and through all and in all.
24 **And put on the new man, which was created ac-**
cording to God in righteousness and holiness of
the reality.

What is the reality of the Body of Christ? In brief, the reality of the Body of Christ is a kind of corporate living, not a living by any individual. This corporate living is the aggregate of many saints who have been redeemed, regenerated, sanctified, and transformed by the processed and consummated God within them. By this indwelling consummated God, these redeemed saints have been made actual God-men. (*The Practical Points concerning Blending,* p. 34)

Today's Reading

Jesus was a genuine man, but He lived not by man's life but by God's life....God's life with all its attributes was lived within this God-man Jesus and expressed as this God-man's virtues.

Such a life was there originally just in an individual man, Jesus Christ. But this life has now been repeated, reproduced, in many men who have been redeemed and regenerated and who now possess the divine life within them. All of them have been nourished, sanctified, transformed, and perfected not just to be matured Christians, but to be God-men. The reality of the Body of Christ is the corporate living by the perfected God-men, who are genuine men but are not living by their life, but by the life of the processed God, whose attributes have been expressed through their virtues.

We come to the highest peak in God's economy—the reality of the Body of Christ. We know the term *the Body of Christ.* We may even have seen the revelation of the Body of Christ. Yet we have to admit that thus far, over the past seventy-two years, through such a long time, we can see very little of the reality of the Body of Christ within us and among us. I am speaking not of the revelation, not even of the vision, but of the reality of the Body of Christ.

This reality has nothing to do with any kind of organization or with anything which remains in the nature of organization. Also, the reality of the Body of Christ is not a system in any way, because no system is organic. The reality of the Body of Christ is absolutely and altogether organic.

To know the purpose of the blending, we need to look into God's eternal economy. Our God, the moving and acting God, made an eternal economy in Himself for Christ in eternity past (Eph. 1:9-10; 3:9-11). In this economy as a plan, an arrangement, God decided to produce an organic Body to be His organism in life for His increase and expression. To carry this out, God Himself had to become a man that man might become God. He accomplished this by the way of union and mingling. Eventually, God and man did unite together and mingle together.

We have the term *the Body of Christ* and we have the doctrine of the Body of Christ, but where is the practicality and reality of the Body of Christ? Have you ever touched the practicality of the Body of Christ? Have you ever been in the reality of the Body of Christ?

We all need to consider this matter. We have the term and we have the doctrine, but practically, we do not have the reality. The purpose of the blending is to usher us all into the reality of the Body of Christ. I treasure the local churches, as you do. But I treasure the local churches because of a purpose. The local churches are the procedure to bring me into the Body of Christ. The churches are the Body, but the churches may not have the reality of the Body of Christ. Thus, we need to be in the local churches so that we can be ushered, or brought, into the reality of the Body of Christ. (*The Practical Points concerning Blending*, pp. 35, 30, 8, 10)

Further Reading: The Practical Points concerning Blending, chs. 1, 4-5

Enlightenment and inspiration: _____

_____

_____

_____

Morning Nourishment

John In that day you will know that I am in My Father,
14:20 and you in Me, and I in you.
23 ...If anyone loves Me, he will keep My word, and
My Father will love him, and We will come to him
and make an abode with him.

The conclusion of the divine revelation in the Bible is a building,
the New Jerusalem. This building is a blending and mingling of divinity with humanity. This is proved by the description of the New
Jerusalem in Revelation 21....The New Jerusalem as the tabernacle of God is for God to dwell in, and God and the Lamb as the temple are for the redeemed saints to dwell in [vv. 3, 22]. This indicates
that the New Jerusalem will be a mutual dwelling place for God
and man. Furthermore, this building is a composition of human
beings. The gates are pearls inscribed with the names of the twelve
tribes of the sons of Israel (v. 12), and on the twelve foundations are
the twelve names of the twelve apostles of the Lamb (v. 14). This
indicates clearly that the New Jerusalem is a composition of the
Triune God, who is the essence, center, and universality, and God's
redeemed people. (*Life-study of 1 & 2 Samuel,* pp. 198-199)

Today's Reading

The New Jerusalem is a composition of divinity and humanity
blended and mingled together as one entity. All the components
have the same life, nature, and constitution and thus are a corporate person. This is a matter of God becoming man and man
becoming God in life and in nature but not in the Godhead. These
two, God and man, man and God, are built up together by being
blended and mingled together. This is the completion, the consummation, of God's building. (*Life-study of 1 & 2 Samuel,* p. 199)

God is moving in the church as a corporate vessel. As such a
vessel the church is the enlargement of Christ, the expansion of
Christ. Now God's move is in a corporate way. This corporate
way is just the Body of Christ, the church, the new man, the
organism of the Triune God.

This stage of God's corporate move is revealed in Acts

through Revelation. This is the deepest and the most profound, heavenly, divine, spiritual, and organic section of the Bible. This section concerns God's eternal economy regarding Christ as the mystery of God (Col. 2:2) and the church, the Body, as the mystery of Christ (Eph. 3:4, 6)....These two mysteries are the contents of the divine economy.

The processed Triune God as the consummated Spirit is in our spirit. Therefore, as Christians we should remain in our spirit. We should not go to visit our flesh, and we should not befriend our soul. Our spirit is our precious place....Here in our spirit we can enjoy the processed Triune God.

We need to learn to exercise our spirit. Exercising our spirit is like breathing. Even when we are resting we are still breathing. We may say that breathing signifies our exercising of our spirit. Just as we breathe without ceasing, we need to pray unceasingly (1 Thes. 5:17). Every time we pray, we need to pray in our spirit (Eph. 6:18). This is spiritual breathing.

In our spiritual breathing by the exercise of our spirit, we enjoy, receive, and absorb the divine substance with the divine essence, the divine element, and the divine expression. This will cause us to be deified, that is, to be constituted with the processed Triune God to be made God in life and in nature but not in the Godhead. In this sense we may speak of the deification of the believers, a process that will consummate in the New Jerusalem.

The New Jerusalem is a composition of God's chosen, redeemed, regenerated, sanctified, transformed, and glorified people who have been deified. On God's side, the Triune God has been incarnated to be a man; on our side, we are being deified, constituted with the processed and consummated Triune God so that we may be made God in life and in nature to be His corporate expression for eternity. This is the highest truth, and this is the highest gospel. (*Life-study of Job,* pp. 120-122)

Further Reading: Life-study of 1 & 2 Samuel, msg. 30; *Life-study of Job,* msg. 22

Enlightenment and inspiration: _____

_____

_____

_____

Hymns, #203

1   In the bosom of the Father,
      Ere the ages had begun,
    Thou wast in the Father's glory,
      God's unique begotten Son.
    When to us the Father gave Thee,
      Thou in person wast the same,
    All the fulness of the Father
      In the Spirit to proclaim.

2   By Thy death and resurrection,
      Thou wast made God's firstborn Son;
    By Thy life to us imparting,
      Was Thy duplication done.
    We, in Thee regenerated,
      Many sons to God became;
    Truly as Thy many brethren,
      We are as Thyself the same.

3   Once Thou wast the only grain, Lord,
      Falling to the earth to die,
    That thru death and resurrection
      Thou in life may multiply.
    We were brought forth in Thy nature
      And the many grains became;
    As one loaf we all are blended,
      All Thy fulness to proclaim.

4   We're Thy total reproduction,
      Thy dear Body and Thy Bride,
    Thine expression and Thy fulness,
      For Thee ever to abide.
    We are Thy continuation,
      Thy life-increase and Thy spread,
    Thy full growth and Thy rich surplus,
      One with Thee, our glorious Head.

Composition for prophecy with main point and sub-points: _____

_____
_____
_____
_____
_____
_____
_____
_____
_____
_____
_____
_____
_____
_____
_____
_____
_____
_____
_____
_____
_____
_____
_____
_____
_____
_____
_____
_____
_____
_____
_____
_____

Living the Life of a God-man
(1)
Being Discipled
to Live the Life of a God-man
to Be Today's Overcomers for a New Revival

Scripture Reading: 1 Pet. 2:21; Matt. 14:19, 22-23; 24:45-51;
John 10:30; 5:19, 30; 7:18; 14:30b *Mark 1 k 22-29*

Day 1 I. God needs a corporate people to be raised
up by His grace through the high peak of the
divine revelation to live a life according to
this revelation:

A. A revival is the practice, the practicality, of the
vision we have seen.

B. If we practice living the life of a God-man, which
is the reality of the Body of Christ, spontaneously a corporate model will be built up, a model
living in the economy of God; this model will be
the greatest revival in the history of the church
to bring the Lord back.

Day 2 II. The disciples of Christ (Matt. 5:1; 28:19) were
discipled through Christ's human living on the
earth, as the model of a God-man, through His
living God by denying Himself in humanity
(John 5:19, 30); this revolutionized their concept concerning man (Phil. 3:10; 1:21a):

A. Our life should be a copy, a reproduction, of the
model of the life of Christ, the first God-man
(1 Pet. 2:21; Matt. 11:28-29; Eph. 4:20-21; John
10:30; 5:19, 30; 7:6, 8, 18).

B. The Spirit of life and reality who was breathed
into the disciples would guide them into the
reality of what they had observed of the Lord
when they were with Him for three and a half
years (16:13; 20:22):

1. At the commencement of the first God-man's
ministry, He was baptized to fulfill all righteousness, recognizing that according to His

flesh (His humanity—1:14; Rom. 1:3; 8:3),
He was good for nothing but death and burial
(Matt. 3:15-17).

Day 3

Wonders

2. He trained His disciples to learn from Him
(11:29) in the miracle of feeding five thousand people with five loaves and two fish:
    a. His looking up to heaven to bless the five
    loaves and the two fish (14:19) indicates
    His realizing that the source of blessing
    was not Him, the sent One, but the Father,
    the sending One.
    b. He did not remain in the issue of the mir-
    acle with the crowds but went away from
    them to be with the Father on the moun-
    tain in prayer (vv. 22-23; Luke 6:12; cf. S. S.
    1:1-4).

Commanding

prayer

3. He taught His disciples to pray to execute
God's will for His economy, having faith in
God without doubting (Matt. 21:21-22; Mark
11:22-24).

4. He lived a life of contacting God (1:35; Luke
5:16; 6:12; 9:28; Heb. 7:25), living in the presence of God without ceasing (Acts 10:38c;
John 8:29; 16:32), and of contacting people,
ministering God into them to bring them into
the jubilee of God's New Testament economy
(Luke 4:18-19; Heb. 8:2; cf. Gen. 14:18; Acts 6:4).

5. He was a man in whom Satan, the ruler of the
world, had nothing (no ground, no chance, no
hope, no possibility in anything) (John 14:30b).

C. We are also discipled to live a God-man life by
observing the intrinsic pattern of Christ's sent
ones, His slaves, who are His duplication; ("I was
in the recovery observing how Brother Watchman Nee acted for eighteen years. All that I observed in him became things discipling me"—
The Vital Groups, p. 18) (1 Cor. 4:17; Heb. 13:7;
Phil. 3:17; 1 Tim. 4:12).

D. The only way to live the life of a God-man according to the Lord's model is to set our entire
being on the mingled spirit, walking, living, and
having our being according to the mingled spirit
(Rom. 8:2, 4, 6, 16; 1 Cor. 6:17; Rom. 10:12; Eph.
6:17-18; 1 Thes. 5:16-20; 2 Tim. 1:6).

Day 4 III. **Matthew 24:45-51 reveals that to live the life
of a God-man we must be faithful to give God
as food to the members of His household so
that we may win Christ as our reward in the
coming kingdom:**

A. God has set faithful and prudent slaves over His
household as household administrators, stew-
ards, channels of supply, to give His people food
at the proper time (1 Tim. 1:4; Matt. 24:45; 1 Cor.
9:17; Eph. 3:2; 1 Cor. 4:1; 1 Pet. 4:10; Phil. 1:25).

B. To give them food refers to ministering the word
of God and Christ as the life supply to the believers in the church; Christ as the life-giving Spirit
is our food, embodied and realized in the word of
life (Matt. 24:45; John 6:57, 63, 68; Acts 5:20):

1. In order to enjoy the Lord as our spiritual
food so that we can feed others, we must pray
over and muse on His word, tasting and
enjoying it through careful considering (Eph.
6:17-18; Psa. 119:15; Ezek. 3:1-4).

2. We must devote ourselves to prayer and the
ministry of the word (Acts 6:4; 2 Cor. 3:6, 8;
John 7:37-39; cf. Heb. 7:25; 8:2).

Day 5 C. To say in our heart that our Master delays is to
love the present evil age and not to love the
Lord's appearing (Matt. 24:48; 2 Tim. 4:8, 10;
cf. Acts 26:16):

1. We must beware of covetousness, not storing
up treasure for ourselves but being rich toward God (Luke 12:16-20; 2 Cor. 6:10; Eph. 3:8).

2. "Remember Lot's wife" is a solemn warning
to the world-loving believers (Luke 17:31-
32; cf. Rom. 1:21, 25).

   3. We must be watchful and beseeching so that
      the day of the Lord's coming would not come
      upon us suddenly as a snare (Luke 21:34-36;
      cf. Matt. 2:3).

Day 6   D. To beat our fellow slaves is to mistreat fellow
      believers (24:49; Acts 9:4):

      1. We must not judge and condemn our fellow
         believers but be kind to them, tenderhearted,
         forgiving them, even as God in Christ forgave
         us (Luke 6:37; Eph. 4:31-32).

      2. We must not revile or criticize our brothers
         but consider them more excellent than our-
         selves (1 Cor. 6:10; Phil. 2:3, 29).

      3. We must not lord it over our fellow believers
         but serve them as slaves to feed them with the
         resurrected Christ as the life-giving Spirit
         (1 Pet. 5:3; Matt. 20:25-28; cf. Num. 17:8).

   E. To eat and drink with the drunken is to keep
      company with worldly people, who are drunk
      with worldly things (Matt. 24:49; cf. Eph. 5:18):

      1. Because of their divine nature and holy
         standing, the believers should not be yoked
         together with the unbelievers; this should
         be applied to all intimate relationships be-
         tween believers and unbelievers, not only to
         marriage and business (2 Cor. 6:14; 1 Cor.
         15:33; cf. Prov. 13:20).

      2. In order to live the life of a God-man, we
         must flee youthful lusts and pursue the all-
         inclusive Christ with those who call on the
         Lord out of a pure heart (2 Tim. 2:22).

IV. **"We should all declare that we want to live
    the life of a God-man. Eventually, the God-
    men will be the victors, the overcomers, the
    Zion within Jerusalem. This will bring in a
    new revival which has never been seen in
    history, and this will end this age"** (*Life-study
    of 1 and 2 Chronicles,* p. 28).

Morning Nourishment

Gal.   I am crucified with Christ; and *it is* no longer I *who*
2:20   live, but *it is* Christ *who* lives in me; and the *life* which I
       now live in the flesh I live in faith, the *faith* of the Son
       of God, who loved me and gave Himself up for me.
Phil. For to me, to live is Christ and to die is gain.
1:21

[All the co-workers and elders] have been called and assigned
by the Lord to carry out God's economy, and God's economy is
altogether centered on Christ, taking Christ as its reality. Without Christ, there is no economy of God. We may be very busy
every day in the Lord's recovery in the church, and we may be
very diligent and faithful, yet we do things which are not the
contents, the reality, and the center of God's economy. (*Living a
Life according to the High Peak of God's Revelation*, p. 30)

Today's Reading

I pray to the Lord, "Lord, grant us in Your recovery to have a
genuine, real revival." We do not want a revival, however, like
the many revivals which went on in the past....What we have
seen of the Lord is in God's central lane, the economy of God,
with Christ as its centrality and universality, with Christ as
its center, reality, and everything. This Christ is now the life-
giving Spirit indwelling our regenerated spirit to be one with
our spirit (1 Cor. 15:45b; 1 Cor. 6:17).

For such a revelation which is so high, deep, and profound,
the Lord needs a model. He needs a corporate people to be raised
up by His grace through this high peak of the divine revelation
to live a life according to this revelation....Where is the model of
living a crucified life that we may live Christ? Even among us,
this is not too prevailing. Where is the model of living Christ and
magnifying Christ by the bountiful supply of the Spirit of Jesus
Christ? Where is this life? We have these revelations released as
messages printed in books, but where is the model?

This is my strong burden I would fellowship with the elders.
Every local church needs this. Do not invent many formalities.
You yourself should practice calling on the Lord. You yourself

should practice pray-reading the word as the Spirit. You need to practice the unceasing prayer. You need to practice never quenching the Spirit, but rather, fanning the Spirit all the time into flame. You need to practice not despising any prophesying. You elders should take the lead to practice this. First, you be the model. Then your practice in such an intimate way with the Lord will influence the saints in your church. Especially as elders, you can exercise much influence over the members of the church.

All the elders and co-workers should pursue this reality so that they will be made into a model by the Lord, a model living in the economy of God. Then they and their churches will become such a model. In my prayer, this is what I call the genuine revival.

Since we have seen such a high peak of the divine revelation, we need to put into practice what we have seen. Our practice will have a success, and that success will be a new revival—the highest revival, and probably the last revival before the Lord's coming back....We need a corporate model, a Body, a people who live the life of a God-man. From today our practice should be to live the life of a God-man by realizing the power of the resurrection of Christ to take His cross as He did, to be crucified, to be conformed to His death, every day to live another One's life (Phil. 3:10; 1:21; Gal. 2:20). Our life, our self, our flesh, our natural man, and our everything were already brought to the cross by Him. Now we are living Him, so we should remain in His crucifixion to be conformed to the mold of His death every moment in every part of our life. That will cause us to spontaneously live Him as the resurrection (John 11:25). This is the living of a God-man.

If we practice what we have heard, spontaneously a model will be built up. This model will be the greatest revival in the history of the church. I believe that this revival will bring the Lord back. (*Living a Life according to the High Peak of God's Revelation,* pp. 30-31, 33, 39-41)

Further Reading: Living a Life according to the High Peak of God's Revelation, chs. 3-5; *The God-man Living,* msgs. 1, 8

Enlightenment and inspiration: _____

_____

_____

_____

Morning Nourishment

Matt. Go therefore and disciple all the nations, baptizing
28:19 them into the name of the Father and of the Son
         and of the Holy Spirit.
John   I can do nothing from Myself; as I hear, I judge, and
5:30   My judgment is just, because I do not seek My own
         will but the will of Him who sent Me.

The constituents of the vital groups are the disciples of Christ
(Matt. 5:1)....The nations [in 28:19] are the Gentiles. To disciple the
Gentiles is to constitute the Gentiles into the disciples of Christ.

The disciples who followed the Lord for three and a half years
saw what He did, how He behaved, and how He spoke. That discipled them....Christ used these three processes—His human
living, His all-inclusive, all-terminating, life-releasing, and new-
man-creating death, and His life-dispensing resurrection—to
disciple His followers. (*The Vital Groups*, pp. 16, 18)

Today's Reading

In Genesis 2 God formed man from the dust of the ground and
breathed into man the breath of life (v. 7). This caused man to become living, that is, a living person. On the day of His resurrection
Christ breathed Himself into His disciples and they also became
living [John 20:22]. They were made alive with the divine life. The
Spirit of life and of reality who was breathed into them would guide
them into all the reality of what they had observed of the Lord
when they were with Him for three and a half years. I was in the
recovery observing how Brother Watchman Nee acted for eighteen
years. All that I observed in him became things discipling me.

The followers of Christ were discipled through Christ's
human living on the earth, as the model of a God-man—living
God by denying Himself in humanity (John 5:19, 30), revolu-
tionizing their concept concerning man (Phil. 3:10; 1:21a). The
concept of the disciples was revolutionized by what they saw of
the Lord Jesus living God by denying Himself in His humanity.

They were discipled through Christ's crucifixion to annul
their human life for them to live the divine life (Gal. 2:20).

They were also discipled through Christ's resurrection to know Him as God's firstborn Son (Rom. 1:4; Acts 13:33; Rom. 8:29). As the only begotten Son of God, Christ had only the divine life and nature. He had nothing human. But as the first-born Son of God, He is both divine and human. Christ had the human life and nature, but He lived the divine life and nature through the denying of His human life and nature. This was His divine and mystical living to disciple all His followers for three and a half years....They were also discipled to know Christ as the life-giving Spirit (1 Cor. 15:45).

Christ's resurrection was for the producing of the many sons of God as His multiplication and increase (Heb. 2:10; John 12:24).

If we open to the Spirit within us as we prayerfully consider this fellowship, we will be discipled....A disciple is one who lives the divine life in his human life. The vitality of the ministry is due to a person's living the divine life out of his human life. Then what he utters is divine out of a crucified human life. We need to deny our human life for the releasing of something divine. This is the main factor of our being vital. (*The Vital Groups,* pp. 18-19)

Before [Christ] carried out any part of His ministry, the first thing He did was to be baptized to fulfill the righteousness according to the way of righteousness brought in by John (Matt. 3:15; 21:32)....No one was righteous, so they all had to repent. When they repented, John baptized them, indicating that they were good only for death and burial.

The Lord Jesus recognized that according to His flesh (His humanity—John 1:14; Rom. 1:3; 8:3) He was good for nothing but death and burial. Jesus needed to be baptized because He became flesh, and the flesh, in the eyes of God, is good for nothing but death and burial. To bury such a dead person by baptism is the way of righteousness, not the way of the law with its statutes and ordinances. (*The God-man Living,* pp. 35-36)

Further Reading: The God-man Living, msgs. 4-6, 13; *The Vital Groups,* msgs. 2-4

Enlightenment and inspiration: _____

_____

_____

_____

Morning Nourishment

Matt. Take My yoke upon you and learn from Me, for I
11:29 am meek and lowly in heart, and you will find rest
for your souls.

14:19 And after commanding the crowds to recline on
the grass, He took the five loaves and the two fish,
and looking up to heaven, He blessed and broke
the loaves and gave *them* to the disciples, and the
disciples to the crowds.

In the performing of the miracle of feeding five thousand people with five loaves and two fish, He trained His disciples to learn from Him. In Matthew 11:29 the Lord told the disciples that they needed to learn from Him, indicating that He was their pattern.

Matthew 14:19 says that He took the five loaves and two fish and when He was going to bless them, He looked up to heaven. In other words, He blessed the food by looking up to heaven. *Looking up to heaven* indicates that He was looking up to His Father in heaven. This indicates that He realized the source of the blessing was not Him. He was the sent One. The sent One should not be the source of blessing. The sending One, the Father, should be the source of blessing. (*The God-man Living*, p. 123)

Today's Reading

Here is a great lesson for us to learn....The Lord...looked up to the Father in heaven and blessed the five loaves and two fish in front of His disciples. After His blessing in this way, He told the disciples what to do. No doubt, what He did was a pattern for the disciples to learn from Him. According to this pattern, we have to realize that we are not the Sender, but the ones sent by the Sender. Regardless of how much we can do, we should realize that we still need the blessing from the source, from our Sender, that we can pass on to the benefited ones.

The Lord did not remain in the issue of the miracle with the crowds but went away from them privately to be with the Father on the mountain in prayer. If we go to a certain place and have a great success, would we leave right away or would we remain in this big success to enjoy it? We need to see and follow the pattern of the Lord Jesus. He did not remain in the issue of the great miracle which He performed. Instead, He went up to the mountain privately to pray. The word *privately* is very meaningful. This means He did not let the people know He was going to pray. Otherwise, they would have followed Him. He went away from them privately to be with the Father in prayer.

The first God-man taught His disciples to pray for executing God's will according to His economy by faith (Matt. 21:21-22).... Thus, the praying one could have faith in God without doubting, but believing that he had received what he asked for, and he would have it (Mark 11:24). The praying one is now one with God, in union with God. He is mingled with God, so God becomes his faith. This is what it means to have faith in God, according to the Lord's word in Mark 11:22. The praying one is absolutely one with God, and God becomes his faith.

In John 14:30 the Lord said, "The ruler of the world is coming, and in Me he has nothing." This means that in the Lord Jesus, Satan as the ruler of the world had no ground, no chance, no hope, no possibility in anything. If we are enlightened, we will admit that Satan has too many things in us. He has the ground, the chance, the hope, and the possibility in many things. But here is a man of prayer,...a man who is one with God, lives in the presence of God continuously, trusts in God in His suffering and persecution, and in whom Satan has nothing. (*The God-man Living,* pp. 123, 127, 144, 90)

As believers in Christ...we must...set our entire being on the mingled spirit. If we will do this, life and peace will be ours, and we will walk, have our being, and do things continually, not only every day but even every moment, in and according to this mingled spirit. (*Living a Life according to the High Peak of God's Revelation,* pp. 23-24)

Further Reading: The God-man Living, msgs. 10, 14, 16; *The Divine and Mystical Realm,* ch. 4

Enlightenment and inspiration: _____

_____

_____

_____

Morning Nourishment

John   Work not for the food which perishes, but for the food
6:27   which abides unto eternal life, which the Son of Man
         will give you; for Him has the Father, *even* God, sealed.
Matt.   Who then is the faithful and prudent slave, whom
24:45-46 the master has set over his household to give them
         food at the proper time? Blessed is that slave whom
         his master, when he comes, will find so doing.

John 6:27 gives us the reason [why the Lord went to the mountain after the miracle of feeding five thousand]....I believe the Lord Jesus went to the mountain to pray in this way: "Father, I pray to You under Your blessing. Through Your blessing You fed the five thousand, but Father, they are just seeking for the food that perishes. I do look unto You that You would bless them that they would seek the food that abides unto eternal life. Father, You know that I am Your sent One. Only I can give them the food that abides unto eternal life, but they do not know Me in this way. They know only that I can perform a miracle to feed them with physical food. But they do not know that it is only I who can give them food that is of the eternal life." (*The God-man Living,* p. 128)

Today's Reading

His going up to the mountain privately to pray indicated His asking the Father to bless all those who had participated in the enjoyment of the issue of the miracle that they would not be satisfied with the food which perishes, but that they should seek for the food which abides unto eternal life and recognize that He was not only the Son of Man but also the Son of God who was sent and sealed by the Father and who could give them eternal life. When the five thousand were being fed by Him, they recognized that He was the capable Son of Man, but they did not realize that He was actually the Son of God who was not only sent but also sealed by the Father. He was the One who could give them the very bread that is related to the eternal life. For this reason, He had another teaching in John 6. In John 6 the Lord revealed that He is the bread out of heaven, the bread of life. Eventually, He told us that this bread is just His word. "The words which I have spoken to you are spirit and are life" (v. 63). John 3:34 says that He is the One who speaks the word and gives the Spirit not by measure. To know Him in this way requires a revelation, so He prayed for them privately on the mountain. (*The God-man Living*, pp. 128-129)

Matthew 24:45 through 51 is concerned with faithfulness and prudence. Verse 45 says, "Who then is the faithful and prudent slave, whom the master has set over his household to give them food at the proper time?" Faithfulness is toward the Lord, whereas prudence is toward the believers. Watchfulness is for rapture into the Lord's presence, but faithfulness is for reigning in the kingdom (v. 47).

The household spoken of in verse 45 refers to the believers (Eph. 2:19), who are the church (1 Tim. 3:15). To give them food is to minister the Word of God with Christ as the life supply to the believers in the church. We all must learn how to minister the life supply to the household of the Lord at the appointed time.

Matthew 24:46 and 47 say, "Blessed is that slave whom his master, when he comes, will find so doing. Truly I say to you that he will set him over all his possessions." To be blessed here is to be rewarded with ruling authority in the manifestation of the kingdom. The faithful slave of the Lord will be set over all His possessions as a reward in the manifestation of the kingdom of the heavens. (*Life-study of Matthew*, pp. 741-742)

Rich in meaning, the Hebrew word for *muse* (often translated *meditate* in the KJV) implies to worship, to converse with oneself, and to speak aloud. To muse on the word is to taste and enjoy it through careful considering. Prayer, speaking to oneself, and praising the Lord may also be included in musing on the word. To muse on the word of God is to enjoy His word as His breath (2 Tim. 3:16) and thus to be infused with God, to breathe God in, and to receive spiritual nourishment. (Psa. 119:15, footnote 1)

Further Reading: Life-study of Matthew, msg. 63

Enlightenment and inspiration: _____

_____

_____

_____

Morning Nourishment

**Matt. But if that evil slave says in his heart, My master
24:48-50 delays, and begins to beat his fellow slaves and
eats and drinks with the drunken, the master of
that slave will come on a day when he does not
expect *him* and at an hour which he does not know.**

[In Matthew 24:48] the evil slave is a believer, because he is
appointed by the Lord (v. 45), he calls the Lord "my master,"
and he believes that the Lord is coming. Verse 49 says that the
evil slave beats his fellow slaves and eats and drinks with the
drunken. To beat the fellow slaves is to mistreat the fellow believers, and to eat and drink with the drunken is to keep company with worldly people, who are drunk with worldly things.
(*Life-study of Matthew*, p. 742)

Today's Reading

Matthew 24:50 and 51 say, "The master of that slave will come
on a day when he does not expect him and at an hour which he
does not know, and will cut him asunder and appoint his portion
with the hypocrites. In that place there will be the weeping and
the gnashing of teeth." The problem with the evil slave is not that
he does not know that the Lord is coming but that he does not
expect Him. He does not like to live the kind of life that is prepared
for the Lord's coming. Therefore, when the Lord comes back, He
will cut him asunder and appoint his portion with the hypocrites.
To cut him asunder means to cut him off. This signifies a separa-
tion from the Lord in His coming glory. This corresponds to being
cast out into the outer darkness in the conclusion of the parable of
the talents (25:14-30), which is a completion to this section. The
Lord will not cut the evil slave in pieces; rather, He will cut him off
from the glory in which He Himself will be. This is equal to being
cast out into outer darkness.

Whoever is cast into outer darkness will be cut off from the
Lord, from His presence, from His fellowship, and from the glorious sphere in which the Lord will be. This is not to perish eternally but to be chastened dispensationally. Who can say that the

evil slave is not a genuine believer? If he were not a brother, how could his work have been assigned by the Lord? The Lord would not assign duties to a false believer. Certainly the evil slave is a saved one. In Matthew, the book of the kingdom, the issue is not salvation. The issue is the kingdom: whether we shall receive a reward to enter into the kingdom, or whether we shall lose the reward, miss the enjoyment of the kingdom, and suffer punishment and discipline where there will be weeping and gnashing of teeth. (*Life-study of Matthew,* pp. 742-743)

The greatest problem today with the Christians is that most of them do not use their gift. I would say that over ninety percent of the genuine Christians today neglect their gift. Of course, this is absolutely due to Catholicism and Protestantism. Because of these two big organizations with their hierarchy and clergy-laity system, most of the believers' gifts and functions have been annulled. They do not use their gifts, and they do not realize that this is a serious mistake that will cause a great loss to them. I feel that we need such a lesson to warn all the saints among us and to stir up their heart to use their gifts.

We need to see that all the members of the Body of Christ are gifted (Rom. 12:6a). In the parables in Matthew 24 and 25, the Lord indicated that every one of His believers has a gift. He did not give the ground for any of His believers to be excused from functioning. All believers are gifted persons.

Matthew 25 tells us that some have five talents, some have two talents, and others have one talent. At the very least, we are the one-talented ones. A saint cannot say that he has not received a talent....We have to convince every saint among us that they cannot say that they do not have any gift and cannot do anything. This is a lie. According to the biblical truth, every believer has a gift. You may have the smallest gift, but you still have a gift. Everyone is talented; everyone is gifted. (*CWWL, 1979,* vol. 2, p. 100)

Further Reading: CWWL, 1979, vol. 2, "Basic Lessons on Service," lsn. 13

Enlightenment and inspiration: _____

_____

_____

_____

Morning Nourishment

Matt. ...That evil slave...begins to beat his fellow slaves
24:48-49 and eats and drinks with the drunken.

Eph. And do not be drunk with wine, in which is disso-
5:18 luteness, but be filled in spirit.

2 Tim. But flee youthful lusts, and pursue righteousness,
2:22 faith, love, peace with those who call on the Lord
out of a pure heart.

Matthew 24 speaks of the evil slave who "says in his heart,
My master delays, and begins to beat his fellow slaves" (vv. 48-49a).
When we mistreat a fellow believer by criticizing, opposing, or
despising him, in the eyes of the Lord, that is to beat him. We
have to say a strong word here. We can easily fall into this danger without any kind of realization. We can fall into criticizing
the brothers and sisters. Sometimes we may oppose or despise
some of the saints. Perhaps we would even fight against them.
This is to beat the Lord's slaves, who are our fellow slaves.
(*CWWL, 1979,* vol. 2, "Basic Lessons on Service," p. 101)

Today's Reading

Matthew 24:49b says that this evil slave "eats and drinks
with the drunken." The Lord's word in Matthew 24 is a parable.
Since it is a parable, it must be interpreted. To eat and drink
with the drunken is to keep company with worldly people, who
are drunk with worldly things. They are drunk with their
worldly enjoyment. This is the danger of not using our gift.
Once we become a person who keeps company with worldly
people, we would not be faithful to the Lord in using the gift He
gives us, so we fall into danger.

In Matthew 25:25 the slothful slave said to his master, "I was
afraid and went off and hid your talent in the earth; behold, you
have what is yours." To be afraid is negative. We should, rather,
be positive and aggressive in using the Lord's gift. To go off and
hide the Lord's talent in the earth is too passive. We should be
active in the Lord's work. If we hide our gift, we do not need to do
anything. To be passive and not active for the Lord's service

means that we are hiding our gift and not using it.

Merely to keep the Lord's gift and not lose it is not sufficient; we must gain a profit by using it....To hide our gift in the earth is not to use it. *The earth* refers to the worldly things. As long as we do not use our gift, we are hiding it.

We have to point out these three dangers: mistreating fellow believers, keeping company with worldly people, and not using our gift to do the Lord's service. We have to point out that many are hiding their gift, not using their gift, because they do not serve.

Ephesians 4:11 speaks of the apostles, prophets, evangelists, and shepherds and teachers. The gifted persons mentioned here are those who have been endued with a special gift. But verse 7 says, "To each one of us grace was given according to the measure of the gift of Christ." *Each one* includes every member of the Body of Christ, each of whom has received a general gift. This shows that everyone is a gifted person and is responsible to use his gift...before the Lord...for the building up of the Body of Christ.

Because we have been regenerated by the Lord, we are gifted. The Lord has given us at least one talent, at least one spiritual gift. If we do not use this gift faithfully, we cannot be in the place that the apostle Paul will be at the Lord's return. A saved person will not suffer eternally in the lake of fire. To say this is an insult to the Lord's redemption and salvation. But a saved believer may suffer some dispensational chastisement in outer darkness. He may be cut off from the Lord's presence in the manifestation of His kingdom. By that time the Lord's presence will be His glory. Thus, the defeated believers will have no share of the Lord's glory in the millennial kingdom.

We need to preach the gospel to the saved ones. This may help some of the brothers and sisters and stir them up to have a real hunger to serve the Lord. We all need to serve the Lord. (*CWWL, 1979,* vol. 2, pp. 101-102, 100-101, 104)

Further Reading: Life-study of 1 & 2 Chronicles, msg. 4

Enlightenment and inspiration: _____

_____

_____

_____

Hymns, #1195

1   Life is mysterious, life is God Himself,
    Whose whole intention focuses on man.
    God made him to take in the tree of life,
    To have a man of life for His own plan.

2   But man was tempted and seduced to sin,
    By taking knowledge from the other source.
    This man then fell as knowledge entered in
    And dominated him with all its force.

3   This knowledge has developed in the man
    Into the human culture on the earth.
    So man, created to fulfill God's plan,
    Became a failure full of Satan's dearth.

4   Then God came in the Person of the Son;
    Lived He on earth, Christ Jesus was His name —
    A living model so that everyone
    Could live by life, God's fullness to obtain.

5   This God-man, Christ, went to the cross and died,
    By death He ended knowledge, the old man.
    Things negative forever crucified,
    Death He subdued, a new life He began!

6   From death He resurrected and became
    The living Spirit to give life to us.
    When we believe and call upon His name;
    This living Spirit comes to dwell in us.

7   By this the very Triune God is now
    The living Spirit mingling deep within.
    Our spirit joins in oneness; this is how
    We are one spirit evermore with Him.

8   'Tis by this Spirit that we walk and act,
    We have our being, think, and see all things;
    We're now within this Spirit! What a fact!
    This Spirit to us all God's fullness brings!

9   So now we have to set our mind on Him;
    Each day, each hour, our mind on Him must be;
    That by this Spirit we'd be saved within
    By life and reign in life eternally.

10 'Tis by this Spirit that we shall be freed
From Sin whose law inside us death would bring.
Our mortal bodies will have life indeed;
Thus sanctified we'll be in everything.

11 This Spirit shall transform our natural life,
Save us from self, build us in one new man,
Till we're conformed to be like Jesus Christ,
Thus finishing our God's eternal plan.

12 Life is our God and life is Christ our Lord.
Life is the Spirit. Life's the only way—
Till we're transfigured and redeemed to God.
We're waiting, looking forward to that day!

Composition for prophecy with main point and sub-points:

practice call the Lord's name — a measure of our living

rescue us from our daily involvement

Living the Life of a God-man
(2)
Living in the Kingdom of God
as the Realm of the Divine Species

Scripture Reading: John 3:3, 5-6; 1:12-13; 2 Pet. 1:4; 1 John 3:1; 2:6

Day 1

I. **The kingdom of God is a realm, not only of the divine dominion but also of the divine species, in which are all the divine things (John 3:3, 5; 18:36):**

A. In John 3 the kingdom of God refers more to the species of God than to the reign of God.

B. God became man to enter into the human species, and man becomes God in life and nature but not in the Godhead to enter into His divine species (1:1, 12-14; 2 Pet. 1:4).

C. In order to enter into the divine realm, the realm of the divine species, we need to be born of God to have the divine life and the divine nature (John 1:12-13; 3:3, 5-6, 15; 2 Pet. 1:4):

   1. God created man, not after man's kind but in His image and according to His likeness to be God's kind, God's species (Gen. 1:26).

   2. The believers, who are born of God by regeneration to be His children in His life and nature but not in His Godhead, are more in God's kind than Adam was (John 1:12-13):

      a. We, the believers in Christ and the children of God, have the reality of the divine life, and we are being transformed and conformed to the Lord's image in our entire being (2 Cor. 3:18; Rom. 12:2; 8:29).

      b. Our second birth, regeneration, caused us to enter into the kingdom of God to become the species of God (John 3:3, 5-6).

D. To be merely a good man is far away from God's good pleasure; we need to realize that, as believ-

ers in Christ, we are God-men in the divine species, children of God possessing the life and nature
of God (Eph. 1:5; 1 John 3:1; John 3:15; 2 Pet. 1:4).

E. To realize that we are God-men, born of God and
belonging to God's species, is the beginning of
the God-man living (1 John 3:1; 2:6).

Day 2   II. **God's intention with Job was that a good**
𝒶𝑔𝒷𝓋   **man would become a God-man (Job 1:1, 8;**
             42:1-6):

A. Job was a good man, expressing himself in his
perfection, uprightness, and integrity (27:5; 31:6;
32:1):

1. Job feared God positively and turned away
from evil negatively (1:1):

   a. God did not create man merely to fear Him
   and to not do anything wrong; rather, God
   created man in His own image and according to His likeness that man may express
   God (Gen. 1:26).

   b. To express God is higher than fearing
   God and turning away from evil.

2. Job did not have God within him; thus, God
wanted Job to gain Him in order to express
Him for the fulfillment of His purpose (Job
42:5-6).

Day 3   B. God's intention was that Job would become a God-
Kom   man, expressing God in His attributes (22:24-25;
             38:1-3):

1. God ushered Job into another realm, the
realm of God, that Job might gain God instead of his attainments in his perfection,
righteousness, and integrity (42:5-6).

Day 4   2. God's intention with Job was to consume
yp   him and to strip him of his attainments, his
             achievements, in the highest standard of
             ethics in perfection and uprightness (31:6).

3. God's intention was to make Job a man of
God, filled with Christ, the embodiment of

God, to be the fullness of God for the expression of God in Christ (1 Tim. 6:11; 2 Tim. 3:17).

4. God's consuming was exercised over Job to tear him down that God might have a base and a way to rebuild him with God Himself, causing Job to become a God-man expressing God (Eph. 3:16-21).

III. **In Christ God has been constituted into man, man has been constituted into God, and God and man have been mingled together to be one entity, which is called the God-man (Matt. 1:21, 23; Luke 1:35; Titus 2:13; 1 Tim. 2:5):**

Day 5

A. Initially, the Bible speaks of the God-man; today this God-man has been reproduced to become the God-men (John 12:24; Rom. 1:3-4; 8:29).

B. The God-men, the sons of God, are the duplication and continuation of Christ, the first God-man (John 12:24; Heb. 2:10; Rom. 8:29).

C. A God-man is one who has been born of God and partakes of God's life and nature, becoming one with God in His life and nature and thereby expressing Him (John 1:12-13; 3:15; 2 Pet. 1:4; 1 Cor. 6:17).

D. A God-man is constituted with God, having God as his life and his everything; a God-man is man yet God and is God yet man (Eph. 3:16-17a).

E. Christ's human living was man living God to express the attributes of God in the human virtues, which were filled, mingled, and saturated with the divine attributes (Luke 1:26-35; 7:11-17; 10:25-37; 19:1-10).

Day 6

F. As the reproduction and duplication of the first God-man, we should live the same kind of life that He lived (1 John 2:6):

1. The Lord's God-man living set up a model for our God-man living—being crucified to live God so that God might be expressed in humanity (Gal. 2:20).

2. We must deny ourselves, be conformed to

Christ's death, and magnify Him by the bountiful supply of His Spirit (Matt. 16:24; Phil. 3:10; 1:10-21a).

3. The One who lives the life of a God-man is now the Spirit living in us and through us; we must reject self-cultivation and the building up of our natural man and allow nothing other than this One to fill us and occupy us so that we may live Him and express Him personally and corporately in the church, which is His Body (Eph. 3:16-19; 1:22-23).

Morning Nourishment

John **Jesus answered and said to him, Truly, truly, I say**
3:3 **to you, Unless one is born anew, he cannot see the**
     kingdom of God.
  5 **Jesus answered, Truly, truly, I say to you, Unless**
     one is born of water and the Spirit, he cannot enter
     into the kingdom of God.

The kingdom of God is the reign of God. This divine reign is a realm, not only of the divine dominion but also of the divine species, in which are all the divine things. The vegetable kingdom is a realm of the vegetable species, and the animal kingdom is a realm of the animal species. In the same way, the kingdom of God is a realm of the divine species. (*Crystallization-study of the Gospel of John,* p. 123)

Today's Reading

God became flesh to enter into the human species, and man becomes God in His life and nature, but not in His divine Godhead, to enter into His divine species. In John 3 the kingdom of God refers more to the species of God than to the reign of God....For something to be in the animal species, it must be born of an animal. Also, to enter into the divine realm, the realm of the divine species, we need to be born of God to have the divine nature and life.

That man was created in the image of God and after His likeness indicates that man was created in God's kind, in God's species. Genesis 1 says that each of the living things was created after its kind. But God created man, not after man's kind, but in God's image and after God's likeness to be God's kind.

The believers, who are born of God by regeneration to be His children in His life and nature but not in His Godhead (John 1:12-13), are more in God's kind than Adam was. Adam had only the outward appearance of God without the inward reality, the divine life. We have the reality of the divine life within us and we are being transformed and conformed to the Lord's image in our entire being. It is logical to say that all the children of God are in the divine realm of the divine species.

Thus, in regeneration God begets gods. Man begets man. Goats beget goats. If goats do not beget goats, what do they beget? If God does not beget gods, what does He beget? If the children of God are not in God's kind, in God's species, in what kind are they? If they are not gods, what are they? We all who are born of God are gods. But for utterance, due to the theological misunderstanding, it is better to say that we are God-men in the divine species, that is, in the kingdom of God.

These God-men, who are children born of God, not only constitute the house of God (1 Tim. 3:15; 1 Pet. 4:17; John 14:2) but also are the constituents with which the Body of Christ is built up, and the Body of Christ will consummate the New Jerusalem as the eternal kingdom of God and of Christ (1 Cor. 6:9; Eph. 5:5; 2 Pet. 1:11; Rev. 11:15). (*Crystallization-study of the Gospel of John*, pp. 123-124)

We must not forget that we are God-men belonging to God's species. As God-men born of God and belonging to God's species, we cannot speak to our spouse in a loose way. A husband must be a God-man, living as a God-man. To be merely a good man is far away from God's good pleasure. We need to see that we are God-men, born of God and belonging to God's species. This is the beginning of the God-man living.

God loves you. God has a good pleasure to make you the same as He is. He is God, so you must be God also. A God-man living is God living. This kind of teaching is much higher than the teaching concerning how to be holy or victorious. In my early days as a believer, I saw many books on how to live the Christian life, but these books did not really reveal the way. How can you be holy? You can be holy by living a God-man life. How can you be victorious? It is only by living a God-man life. Never forget that you are a God-man, born of God and belonging to God's species. (*The God-man Living*, p. 9)

Further Reading: Crystallization-study of the Gospel of John, msg. 12; *The God-man Living*, ch. 1

Enlightenment and inspiration: _____

_____

_____

_____

Morning Nourishment

Job There was a man in the land of Uz whose name was
1:1 Job; and this man was perfect and upright, and he
     feared God and turned away from evil.
  8 And Jehovah said to Satan, Have you considered
     My servant Job? For there is none like him on the
     earth, a perfect and upright man, who fears God
     and turns away from evil.

In the book of Job, thirty-five chapters, 3—37, are a record of the words spoken by Job, his three friends, and Elihu. All of these five persons are God-fearing and God-seeking people, but the words spoken by them in the book of Job are very much according to their concepts concerning God's will for man, their understanding of the meaning of human life, and their realization concerning the perfection of human virtues, all of which contradict God's purpose in man, that is, that man should be filled with God to express God rather than all other things, including man's perfection of human virtues. Hence, God stripped Job of his uprightness and integrity that he might seek God Himself instead of anything else. Yet their words, which are against God's will in man, are written by them under the inspiration of the Spirit of God to serve the purpose of God to expose the mistake of Job, his three friends, and Elihu in knowing God that man may be enlightened to realize that, according to God's good pleasure of His heart's desire, man should be the expression of God only, rather than the expression of man's perfection of his uprightness and integrity. (*Crystallization-study of the Epistle of James*, pp. 87-88)

Today's Reading

In addition to being perfect inwardly and upright outwardly, Job feared God positively and turned away from evil negatively. However, even with the positive matter of fearing God, there is not anything that is actually positive. God did not create man merely to fear Him without doing anything wrong. The Bible tells us that God created man in His own image and after His likeness that man may express Him (Gen. 1:26). This is the most positive thing among all positive things. To fear God and turn away from evil is not adequate, and actually this is not positive. The most positive thing is to express God. To express God is higher than fearing God and turning away from evil.

Job's sons would hold feasts in each one's house, each on his own day, and they would invite their sisters to eat and drink with them (Job. 1:4). Job would send word and sanctify them, and he would rise early in the morning and offer burnt offerings for them, saying, "Perhaps my children have sinned and have cursed God in their heart" (v. 5). Because feasting, an excess in eating, can be worldly, Job sanctified his children after their days of feasting....He surely was a godly father.

Ethically speaking, Job was very good. According to human eyes, there was no problem with Job. God even boasted to Satan regarding how good Job was (v. 8; 2:3). Only God knew that Job had a need, that he was short of God. Because of His loving concern for Job, God held a council in the heavens to talk about Job.

Job had been laboring under God's blessing for many years, and he had accumulated many things. He had seven thousand sheep, three thousand camels, five hundred yoke of oxen, five hundred female donkeys, and a great many servants. He had a dear wife and seven sons and three daughters. Moreover, Job was very successful in being perfect and upright and in holding to his integrity. His possessions, success, and attainment made him a contented and satisfied person. Although Job was full of possessions and full of his attainment, he did not have God within him. As God looked upon Job, He might have said, "Job, what shall I do with you? You are full of your possessions and your attainment, but you are not full of Me. You have Me in name, but you do not have Me within you." Thus, for God's dealing with Job, Satan was needed. Satan was the unique one in the universe who could and who would fulfill God's intention of stripping Job of his possessions and his ethical attainment. (*Life-study of Job*, pp. 9-12)

Further Reading: Life-study of Job, msgs. 2-4

Enlightenment and inspiration: _____

_____

_____

_____

Morning Nourishment

Job | Let Him weigh me in a righteous balance, and let
31:6 | God know my integrity.
42:5-6 | I had heard of You by the hearing of the ear, but now my eye has seen You; therefore I abhor *myself*, and I repent in dust and ashes.

In God's appearing to Job (Job 38:1-3; 40:1-14), His intention was to show Job that he was nothing and that God is unlimited, unsearchable, and untraceable. God's appearing also implied that He wanted to help Job to know that he was in the wrong realm, the realm of building up himself as a man in the old creation in his perfection, uprightness, and integrity. Job glorified himself in these things, but God considered them frustrations to be stripped away so that Job might receive God in His nature, life, element, and essence and thus be metabolically transformed to be a God-man, a man in the new creation who expresses God and dispenses Him to others. (Job 38:1, footnote 1)

Today's Reading

God's dealing with Job in all the disasters and His stripping him of all that he was, were to take away his contentment in his godly attainments and obtainments and to remove all the barriers and coverings so that he could be emptied for some further seeking after God and could realize that what he was short of in his human life was God Himself. At the end of the book of Job, God came in to reveal Himself to Job, indicating that He Himself was what Job should pursue, gain, and express. In all God's dealings with Job, God's intention was to reduce Job to nothing, yet to maintain his existence (Job 2:6) so that He might have time to impart Himself into Job. (Job 38:1, footnote 1)

In the New Testament sense, seeing God equals gaining God. To gain God is to receive God in His element, in His life, and in His nature that we may be constituted with God. All God's redeemed, regenerated, sanctified, transformed, conformed, and glorified people will see God's face (Rev. 22:4). Seeing God transforms us (2 Cor. 3:18; cf. 1 John 3:2), because in seeing God we receive His element into us and our old element is discharged. This metabolic process is transformation (Rom. 12:2). To see God is to be transformed into the glorious image of Christ, the God-man, that we may express God in His life and represent Him in His authority. (Job 42:5, footnote 1)

The more we see God, know God, and love God, the more we abhor ourselves and the more we deny ourselves (Matt. 16:24; Luke 9:23; 14:26). (Job 42:6, footnote 1)

Job was right in saying that his sufferings were not a matter of God's judgment. Job felt that, according to his conscience, he had not done anything that required God to judge him or to punish him. Nevertheless, he was suffering and he wanted to investigate his situation with God. Job's three friends, however, insisted that Job's sufferings were a proof that he had done something wrong and was being judged by God. Thus, God came in to condemn the three friends and to vindicate Job to a certain extent.

Nevertheless, Job was devoid of the divine revelation, not knowing that God's purpose in dealing with His people is that He wants His people to gain Him, to partake of Him, to possess Him, and to enjoy Him, rather than all things, until their enjoyment reaches the fullest extent (Phil. 3:7-14; 2 Cor. 4:16-17), as the divine revelation ultimately unveils in the New Testament, that His people may ultimately become the New Jerusalem (Rev. 21:2—22:5). (Job 42:7, footnote 1)

Even today, after God deals with us by stripping us and consuming us, and after His purpose is accomplished, God gives us His physical blessings. However, God's purpose in dealing with His people is not to give physical blessings to them but to give Himself to them as their eternal portion, which ultimately consummates in the New Jerusalem. The all-embracing aggregate, the totality, of the divine blessing given by God to His people is the all-inclusive life-giving Spirit as the consummation of the processed Triune God (Gal. 3:14). (Job 42:10, footnote 1)

Further Reading: Life-study of Job, msgs. 24, 30

Enlightenment and inspiration: _____

_____

_____

_____

Morning Nourishment

1 Tim. But you, O man of God, flee these things, and pur-
6:11   sue righteousness, godliness, faith, love, endurance,
        meekness.
Eph.   That Christ may make His home in your hearts
3:17   through faith, that you, being rooted and grounded
        in love.

God's intention with Job was to consume this "perfect and upright" person and to strip his attainments, his achievements, in the highest standard of ethics in perfection and uprightness (Job 1:1)....God's intention was also to tear down the natural Job in his perfection and uprightness that He might build up a renewed Job in God's nature and attributes....God's intention was not to have a Job in the line of the tree of the knowledge of good and evil but a Job in the line of the tree of life (Gen. 2:9). (*Life-study of Job,* p. 29)

Today's Reading

Eventually, God's intention was to make Job a man of God (1 Tim. 6:11; 2 Tim. 3:17), filled with Christ, the embodiment of God, to be the fullness of God for the expression of God in Christ, not a man of the high standard of ethics in Job's natural perfection, natural uprightness, and natural integrity, which Job attempted to maintain and hold (Job 2:3, 9a). Such a person, constituted with God according to His economy, would never be entangled by any troubles and problems so that he would curse his birth and prefer to die rather than to live.

I am happy that we are now studying the book of Job. However, I am somewhat concerned that we may come to this book merely to gain more knowledge. We may condemn the tree of the knowledge of good and evil, but we may add to the growth of the tree of knowledge by picking up mere knowledge from our study of Job.

We need to see that the entire Bible is a book on God's eternal economy. In His economy God's intention is to dispense Himself into us to be our life and our nature that we may be the same as He is in life and nature in order to express Him. What, then, about the stripping and the consuming? God's stripping and

God's consuming are to tear us down. We are fallen and natural men. As such men, we need to be torn down. God must tear us down. Then God can have a base, a way, to build us up again.

Many Christians think that fallen man needs help so that he can be made whole. However, in His economy God's intention is not to make fallen man whole. Rather, God's intention is to tear us down and rebuild us with Himself as our life and our nature that we may be persons who are absolutely one with Him.

The book of Job shows us that God, through Satan as an ugly tool, was tearing Job down by two ways: stripping and consuming. God's stripping and consuming were exercised over Job to tear Job down that God might have a base and a way to rebuild him with God Himself that he might become a God-man. This is what we should receive in our study of Job. (*Life-study of Job*, pp. 29, 34-35)

The vast majority of today's Christians neglect the crucial point in the Bible that in Christ God has become man in order to make man God in life and in nature but not in the Godhead and that God desires to mingle Himself with man to be one entity.

What is revealed in 2 Samuel 7 is expounded by Paul in Romans 1:3-4, where he tells us that Christ, a descendant of David, has been designated the Son of God. These verses say, "Concerning His Son, who came out of the seed of David according to the flesh, who was designated the Son of God in power according to the Spirit of holiness out of the resurrection of the dead, Jesus Christ our Lord." Christ is a descendant of David, yet He has been designated to be the Son of God. This is the mystery of God becoming man to make man God in life and in nature but not in the Godhead. The two, God and man, are thus built together, constituted into each other. In Christ God has been constituted into man, man has been constituted into God, and God and man have been mingled together to be one entity, which is called the God-man. (*Life-study of 1 & 2 Samuel*, pp. 204-205)

Further Reading: Life-study of Job, msgs. 31, 33

Enlightenment and inspiration: _____

_____

_____

_____

Morning Nourishment

Matt. And she will bear a son, and you shall call His
1:21 name Jesus, for *it is* He *who* will save His people
from their sins.
23 "Behold, the virgin shall be with child and shall
bear a son, and they shall call His name Emmanuel" (which is translated, God with us).

Initially, the Bible speaks of the God-man. Today this God-man has become the God-men. The God-man is Jesus Christ, who is God incarnated to be a man. As such a One, He is the God-man. Furthermore, He is the model God-man, the prototype for the producing of many God-men (Rom. 1:3-4; 8:29), including all the dear saints throughout the world. Regardless of our nationality, and regardless of whether we are male or female, young or old, we all must believe that we are God-men. We are all God-men, and each one of us is a God-man. (*The God-men,* p. 10)

Today's Reading

Our God was merely God up to two thousand years ago. Then He became a man. Of course, He did not drop His divinity. He was still God. Thus, the man Jesus was a God-man. He went through human living, death, and resurrection and entered into ascension. After His ascension He is still the God-man, and through His death and resurrection, many God-men were reproduced.

The New Jerusalem is the aggregate, the totality, of many God-men. Among these many God-men, the sons of God, is the Father. Christ is the firstborn Son and we are His many "twins." The New Jerusalem is God the Father with many "God the sons."...I believe that in the New Jerusalem, God the Father will look at "God the sons," and He will be very happy. We will be there as the many God-men. In the New Jerusalem, the Father will be the unique One, and all the others will be the sons. (*The Practical Way to Live a Life according to the High Peak of the Divine Revelation in the Holy Scriptures,* p. 37)

A man of God [2 Tim. 3:17] is a God-man, one who partakes of God's life and nature (John 1:13; 2 Pet. 1:4), thus being one with

God in His life and nature (1 Cor. 6:17) and thereby expressing Him. Such a God-man, such a man of God, is produced by God's breathing out of Himself. God's breathing produces God-men. (*Teacher's Training,* pp. 14-15)

Christ's entering into glory is the proof of God's accomplished redemption (Luke 24:26; Rom. 4:25). The person in glory in the heavens is both God and man; He is man yet God, and God yet man. The resurrection of Christ from the dead signaled the accomplishment of God's eternal plan by issuing in a person who is God mingled with man and man joined with God. This is the result that God intended to obtain in eternity past, and it is the issue of His work in time. Hence, God's heart is full of joy.

A person who sets up a factory to mass-produce a certain product must first produce a prototype. After he has successfully produced a prototype, he can begin to mass-produce the prototype....The resurrected and glorified Christ, who is God yet man, is the prototype of God's redemptive work. He is the issue of God's redemptive work. God can now work to mass-produce Christ as the prototype. (*Redemption in God's Plan,* p. 102)

As the Son of Man, Christ has all the virtues of humanity (Psa. 45:2a). The Lord Jesus possesses both the divine nature with its divine attributes and the human nature with its human virtues. In Him we see all the attributes of God and all the human virtues, for His constitution is a composition of the divine nature with its divine attributes and the human nature with its human virtues. Moreover, in Christ the divine attributes strengthen and enrich the human virtues. With Him the divine attributes fill the human virtues, and the human virtues contain the divine attributes. The divine attribute is the inward reality, and the human virtue is the outward appearance. Therefore, the virtues of the man Jesus are filled, mingled, and saturated with the attributes of God. (*The Conclusion of the New Testament,* p. 2773)

Further Reading: Life-study of Mark, msgs. 52-63; *Life-study of Luke,* msg. 61

Enlightenment and inspiration: _____

_____

_____

_____

Morning Nourishment

Phil. For I know that for me this will turn out to salvation
1:19-21 through your petition and *the* bountiful supply of
the Spirit of Jesus Christ, according to my earnest
expectation and hope that in nothing I will be put
to shame, but with all boldness, as always, even
now Christ will be magnified in my body, whether
through life or through death. For to me, to live is
Christ and to die is gain.

Many Christians know that one day God was incarnated to be
a man by the name of Jesus. They know this just in black and
white, but sorry to say, they do not know the intrinsic fact of this
incarnation. This incarnation produced a God-man, who lived on
the earth not by His human life but by His divine life. All the days
when He was on earth, He put Himself on the cross. He remained
on the cross to die that He might live by God, not to express man
but to express God in His divine attributes becoming man's virtues. This was the life of the first God-man as a prototype. Today
we are His reproduction, His many copies, so we should live the
same kind of life. (*The Practical Way to Live a Life according to the
High Peak of the Divine Revelation in the Holy Scriptures,* p. 25)

Today's Reading

First Peter 2:21…tells us that Christ in His human living left
us a model, an example, for us to copy. Christ Jesus, while He
was on this earth, set up a copy for spiritual xeroxing. He was the
model, the copy, for xeroxing, to produce millions of copies. (*The
Practical Way to Live a Life according to the High Peak of the
Divine Revelation in the Holy Scriptures,* p. 15)

The way for the God-men to be the overcomers is first to love
Christ and follow Him (John 21:15-17, 19b). The God-men as the
overcomers must also pursue Christ and gain Him (Phil. 3:12-15),
and they must be conformed to the death of Christ by the power of
His resurrection (v. 10). In everything we need to be conformed to
Christ's death. In everything we should be crucified. It should be
"no longer I," because the "I" has been crossed out (Gal. 2:20a). In

ourselves it is impossible for us to be conformed to Christ's death. However, we do have the resurrected Christ living within us. We should rely on the power of His resurrection that we may be conformed to His death in everything. Many times I realized that I was not conformed to the Lord's death in my attitude toward my wife. After speaking just one short sentence in an unpleasant tone, I realized that I was not conformed to the death of Christ. I have repented for such sins nearly every day for many years.

The overcomers also need to live Christ and magnify Him by the bountiful supply of His all-inclusive Spirit (Phil. 1:19-21). Today the Spirit is not only the Spirit of God but also the Spirit of Jesus Christ, who has the bountiful supply for us to live Christ and magnify Christ. (*The God-men,* pp. 44-45)

In their reading of the Proverbs and even of the entire Bible, many Christians receive only teachings, admonitions, exhortations, proverbs, and precepts to cultivate their self and to build up the natural man, who has been fully condemned by God. We must learn to come to the Word of God as those who are approaching God, not to receive proverbs and teachings but to receive nourishment and enlightenment, so that we may know that, according to God, we should always be conformed to the death of Christ by the power of His resurrection (Phil. 3:10), which is the consummated Spirit, who is the reality of the resurrection of Christ.

We must reject self-cultivation and condemn the building up of the natural man. We need to turn the Bible from a book that teaches us to cultivate the self and to build up the natural man to a book that is full of life, spirit, spiritual nourishment, and spiritual enlightenment. This will tear down our self, break our natural man, and supply us with the consummated Spirit of the Triune God. Then we will live a life not by our natural man, by our old man, and by our self but by the Lord Jesus, who is our life and person living in our spirit. (*Life-study of Proverbs,* pp. 28-29)

Further Reading: Life-study of Proverbs, msgs. 6, 8; *Life-study of Mark,* msgs. 66-67

Enlightenment and inspiration: _____

_____

_____

_____

Hymns, #403

1   Live Thyself, Lord Jesus, through me,
     For my very life art Thou;
   Thee I take to all my problems
     As the full solution now.
   Live Thyself, Lord Jesus, through me,
     In all things Thy will be done;
   I but a transparent vessel
     To make visible the Son.

2   Consecrated is Thy temple,
     Purged from every stain and sin;
   May Thy flame of glory now be
     Manifested from within.
   Let the earth in solemn wonder
     See my body willingly
   Offered as Thy slave obedient,
     Energized alone by Thee.

3   Every moment, every member,
     Girded, waiting Thy command;
   Underneath the yoke to labor
     Or be laid aside as planned.
   When restricted in pursuing,
     No disquiet will beset;
   Underneath Thy faithful dealing
     Not a murmur or regret.

4   Ever tender, quiet, restful,
     Inclinations put away,
   That Thou may for me choose freely
     As Thy finger points the way.
   Live Thyself, Lord Jesus, through me,
     For my very life art Thou;
   Thee I take to all my problems
     As the full solution now.

Composition for prophecy with main point and sub-points: _____

_____

_____

_____

_____

_____

_____

_____

_____

_____

_____

_____

_____

_____

_____

_____

_____

_____

_____

_____

_____

_____

_____

_____

_____

_____

_____

_____

_____

_____

_____

_____

_____

Shepherding according to God
(1)
Shepherding People by Cherishing
and Nourishing Them
according to the Pattern
of the Lord Jesus and of the Apostle Paul

Scripture Reading: John 10:11; Heb. 13:20; 1 Pet. 5:4; Eph.
5:29; John 21:15-17; Acts 20:20, 28, 31; 2 Cor. 11:28-29;
1 Cor. 9:22; 2 Cor. 12:15; 1 Cor. 8:1; 13:4-8a

Day 1
I. **We need to shepherd people according to the
pattern of the Lord Jesus in His ministry for
carrying out God's eternal economy (Matt.
9:36; John 10:11; Heb. 13:20; 1 Pet. 5:4):**
A. The content of God's entire New Testament economy in His complete salvation is Christ as the
Son of Man cherishing us and as the Son of God
nourishing us (Eph. 5:29):
1. Christ as the Son of Man came to redeem us
from sin, accomplishing His judicial redemption through His death (1 Tim. 1:15; Eph.
1:7)—cherishing.
2. Christ as the Son of God came to impart the
divine life into us abundantly, carrying out
His organic salvation in His resurrection
(John 10:10; 1 Cor. 15:45b)—nourishing.

Day 2
B. In Luke 15 the Lord Jesus unveiled the saving
love of the Triune God for sinners (vv. 1-2):
1. We need to follow the steps of the processed
Triune God in seeking and gaining fallen people (vv. 3-7, 8-10, 17-18).
2. Our not having the Father's loving and forgiving heart and the Savior's shepherding and
seeking spirit is the reason for our barrenness.
3. We need to cherish people (to make them
happy and to make them feel pleasant and
comfortable) in the humanity of Jesus (Matt.
9:10; Luke 7:34).

4. We need to nourish people (to feed them with the all-inclusive Christ in His ministry of three stages) in the divinity of Christ (Matt. 24:45-47).

Day 3
C. Christ came not as a Judge but as a Physician to heal, recover, enliven, and save the lepers (8:2-4), paralytics (vv. 5-13; 9:2-8), the fever-ridden (8:14-15), the demon-possessed (vv. 16, 28-32), those ill with all kinds of diseases (v. 16), despised tax collectors, and sinners (9:9-11) that they might become reconstituted to become people of His heavenly kingdom (vv. 12-13).

D. He had to pass through Samaria, purposely detouring to Sychar to gain one immoral woman, cherishing her by asking her to give Him something to drink that He might nourish her with the flowing Triune God as the water of life (John 4:3-14).

E. As the One without sin, He did not condemn the adulterous woman but cherished her for the forgiveness of her sins judicially and for the setting free from her sins organically (8:1-11, 32, 36).

F. He went to Jericho just to visit and gain one person, a chief tax collector, and His preaching was a shepherding (Luke 19:1-10).

G. He cherished the parents by laying His hands on their children (Matt. 19:13-15).

Day 4
H. The first one saved by Christ through His crucifixion was a robber sentenced to death (Luke 23:42-43).

I. The Lord's commissioning Peter to feed His lambs and shepherd His sheep was to incorporate the apostolic ministry with His heavenly ministry to take care of God's flock, which is the church that issues in the Body of Christ (John 21:15-17; Heb. 13:20; 1 Pet. 5:1-4; 2:25; cf. Heb. 13:17):

1. In His heavenly ministry, Christ as the High Priest, with a golden girdle on His breast, is cherishing and nourishing the churches (Rev. 1:12-13).

2. In His heavenly ministry, Christ is the Great Shepherd of the sheep to consummate the New Jerusalem according to God's eternal covenant (Heb. 13:20-21).

Day 5 **II. We need to shepherd people according to the pattern of the apostle Paul as a good shepherd, taking care of God's flock (1 Tim. 1:16; Acts 20:28):**

A. Paul shepherded the saints as a nursing mother and an exhorting father (1 Thes. 2:7-8, 11-12).

B. Paul shepherded the saints in Ephesus by teaching them "publicly and from house to house" (Acts 20:20) and by admonishing each one of them with tears even for as long as three years (vv. 31, 19), declaring to them all the counsel of God (v. 27).

C. Second Corinthians 3:2-3 reveals that Paul wrote living letters of Christ with the life-giving Spirit as the essence:

1. Because the believers are a letter of Christ, they are also the letter inscribed in the heart of the apostles; today while we are ministering Christ to others, Christ is simultaneously written in the one to whom we are ministering and also in us.

2. This means that we can never forget those to whom we have ministered Christ; the one writing produces two original copies and involves two hearts becoming one.

D. Paul had an intimate concern for the believers (7:3; Philem. 7, 12).

E. He came down to the weak ones' level so that he could gain them (2 Cor. 11:28-29; 1 Cor. 9:22; cf. Matt. 12:20).

Day 6 F. He was willing to spend what he had, referring to his possessions, and to spend what he was, referring to his being, for the sake of the saints (2 Cor. 12:15).

G. He was a drink offering, one with Christ as the wine producer, sacrificing himself for others' enjoyment of Christ (Phil. 2:17; Judg. 9:13; Eph. 3:2).

H. He was a minister of the Spirit to honor God by being filled with the Spirit to walk by the Spirit for His glory and to honor man by ministering the Spirit to them for their supply (2 Cor. 3:6, 8; Gal. 5:16, 25; Judg. 9:9).

I. Paul indicated in his teaching that the church is a home to raise up people, a hospital to heal and recover them, and a school to teach and edify them (Eph. 2:19; 1 Thes. 5:14; 1 Cor. 14:31).

J. Paul revealed that love is the most excellent way for us to be anything and to do anything for the building up of the Body of Christ (8:1; 12:31; 13:4-8a).

III. "I hope that there will be a genuine revival among us by our receiving this burden of shepherding. If all the churches receive this teaching to participate in Christ's wonderful shepherding, there will be a big revival in the recovery" (*The Vital Groups*, p. 40).

Morning Nourishment

Luke   Now all the tax collectors and sinners were drawing
15:1-2 near to Him to hear Him. And both the Pharisees and
         the scribes murmured among *themselves,* saying, This
         man welcomes sinners and eats with them.
John   ...I have come that they may have life and may
10:10-11 have *it* abundantly. I am the good Shepherd; the
         good Shepherd lays down His life for the sheep.

The content of God's entire New Testament economy is
Christ as the Son of Man cherishing us and as the Son of God
nourishing us....The Jesus who is portrayed in the four Gospels
is very cherishing. He came to the world just to cherish people.
All people need Him to cherish them, to make them happy,
comfort them, and give them rest. If He came to us in His divine
status, this would intimidate us. But even the most sinful tax
collectors could sit with Him as friends, eating and talking with
Him (Luke 15:1; Matt. 9:10). The scribes and Pharisees, the self-
justified ones, could not bear to see Him eating with tax collectors and sinners. They did not realize that they also needed Him
to be their Physician....The four Gospels reveal Christ as the
cherishing Son of Man to meet the need of every fallen sinner. If
you are sick of leprosy, He will cleanse you. If you are blind, He
will give you sight. This is the Jesus in the four Gospels. (*The
Vital Groups,* pp. 80-81)

Today's Reading

The full ministry of Christ is in three stages: incarnation,
inclusion, and intensification. His ministry in the first stage of
incarnation was to cherish people, to draw and attract people to
Him. Once He was walking in a pressing crowd, and a sick woman
desperately touched the fringe of His garment and was healed
(Matt. 9:20-22). Everyone needs Him, can approach Him, and can
touch Him. No one who came to Him was rejected by Him. He
receives all without preference or discrimination.

His visiting was His cherishing. His death on the cross was the
biggest cherishing to redeem us. Without His redemption, who

could come to Him? When we heard the story of His death on the cross, our tears came down. We were attracted by Him.

In resurrection He was transfigured to become the life-giving Spirit, the Spirit of the bountiful supply (1 Cor. 15:45b; Phil. 1:19). This Spirit is for nourishing. As the all-inclusive Spirit from Acts through the Epistles, Christ nourishes us. This nourishing produces the church, builds up the Body of Christ, and will consummate the New Jerusalem. Because of the church's degradation, Christ's nourishing becomes sevenfold intensified in the book of Revelation to bring forth the eternal goal of God, the New Jerusalem. The totality of His nourishing will be this great universal city, which is the enlargement and expression of God. This city is the consummation of the bountiful supply of Christ as the life-giving, sevenfold intensified Spirit for nourishing us. The New Testament is composed of just two sections—cherishing and nourishing. With this revelation the entire New Testament has become a new book to me.

God sent His Son as a propitiation for our sins in His humanity (1 John 4:10)—cherishing. As the Son of Man, Christ came to be the sin offering to appease the situation between the sinners and God....God sent His Son to us that we may have life and live through Him in His divinity (1 John 4:9)—nourishing. This is confirmed by John 3:16: God gave us His only begotten Son that we who believe into Him may not perish through His redemption in His humanity (cherishing) but may have eternal life in His divinity (nourishing). God gave His only begotten Son to redeem us in His humanity judicially so that we may have eternal life in His divinity for Him to save us organically.

Christ as the Son of Man came to redeem us from sin (1 Tim. 1:15)—cherishing. This is the first part of the New Testament.

Christ as the Son of God came to impart the divine life into us abundantly (John 10:10)—nourishing. This is the second part of the New Testament. (*The Vital Groups*, pp. 82, 86-87)

Further Reading: The Vital Groups, msgs. 6, 9, 14

Enlightenment and inspiration: _____
_____
_____
_____

Morning Nourishment

Luke   Which man of you, who has a hundred sheep and
15:4-5 has lost one of them, does not leave the ninety-nine
in the wilderness and go after the one which is lost
until he finds it? And when he finds *it*, he lays *it* on
his shoulders, rejoicing.

We have to follow the steps of the processed Triune God in
His seeking and gaining fallen people....[In Luke 15] the Lord
told three wonderful parables, which unveil the saving love of
the Triune God toward sinners.

The Son as the shepherd would leave the ninety-nine to
seek the one lost sheep (Luke 15:3-7).

The second parable is that of a woman seeking a lost coin
(vv. 8-10). This signifies the Spirit seeking a lost sinner. The
Son's finding took place outside the sinner and was completed
at the cross through His redemptive death. The Spirit's seeking is inward and is carried out by His working within the re-
penting sinner. (*The Vital Groups,* p. 39)

Today's Reading

Because of the Son's step of seeking the sinner by dying on
the cross and the Spirit's step of sanctifying by searching and
cleansing the sinner's inward parts, the sinner comes to his
senses. This is shown by the prodigal son's coming to himself
and desiring to return to his father (Luke 15:17-18). First Peter
1:2 reveals that before we received the sprinkling of Christ's
blood, the Holy Spirit sanctified us. This is His seeking sanctification. The sinner is awakened by the Spirit's seeking to cause
him to return to the Father. When the prodigal son returned,
his father saw him while he was still a long way off. This indicates that the father was expectantly waiting and watching day
by day for his son to return. When his father saw him, he ran to
receive his returning son (Luke 15:20). This shows that God
the Father runs to receive the returning sinners.

I believe there will be a big revival on the earth, not by a few
spiritual giants but by the many members of Christ's Body being

shepherds who follow the steps of the processed Triune God in seeking and gaining fallen people. (*The Vital Groups,* pp. 39-40)

I believe that not having the Father's loving and forgiving heart and not having the Savior's shepherding and seeking spirit is the reason for our barrenness. I realize that you all work hard, but there is almost no fruit....A good, gentle pastor may not have a particular gift, such as the gift of speaking; he may simply visit people and welcome them when they come to his meeting, but according to statistics, he will have a ten-percent yearly increase. We, however, do not have even a ten-percent increase. Can you see how barren we are? Many of you are good speakers, knowing the higher truths....However, we do not have fruit because we are lacking in the Father's loving and forgiving heart and the Son's shepherding and seeking spirit. We condemn and regulate others rather than shepherd and seek them. We are short of love and shepherding. These are the vital factors for us to bear fruit, that is, to gain people....Do we train the young ones to gain people or to regulate people? We have to reconsider our ways, as Haggai said (Hag. 1:5). Our way is not right; something is wrong. (*A Word of Love to the Co-workers, Elders, Lovers, and Seekers of the Lord,* pp. 40-41)

To cherish people is to make them happy and to make them feel pleasant and comfortable. We must have a pleasant countenance when we contact people. We should be happy and rejoicing. We should not contact anyone with a cheerless countenance. We must give people the impression that we are genuinely happy and pleasant. Otherwise, we will not be able to cherish them, to make them happy.

Then we should go on to nourish them. We do not nourish people when we speak to them about marriage, courtship, politics, the world situation, or education. To nourish people is to feed them with the all-inclusive Christ in His full ministry in three stages. (*The Vital Groups,* pp. 102-103)

Further Reading: The Vital Groups, msg. 4; A Word of Love to the Co-workers, Elders, Lovers, and Seekers of the Lord, chs. 2-3

Enlightenment and inspiration: _____

_____

_____

_____

Morning Nourishment

Matt. ...When He heard *this*, He said, Those who are strong
9:12 have no need of a physician, but those who are ill.
John But whoever drinks of the water that I will give
4:14 him shall by no means thirst forever; but the water
that I will give him will become in him a fountain
of water springing up into eternal life.

In calling people to follow Him for the kingdom, the King of the
heavenly kingdom ministered as a Physician, not as a Judge. A
judge's judgment is according to righteousness, whereas a physician's healing is according to mercy and grace. Those whom He
made people of His heavenly kingdom were lepers (Matt. 8:2-4),
paralytics (8:5-13; 9:2-8), the fever-ridden (8:14-15), the demon-
possessed (8:16, 28-32), those ill with all kinds of diseases (8:16),
despised tax collectors, and sinners (9:9-11). If He had visited
these pitiful people as a Judge, all would have been condemned
and rejected, and none would have been qualified, selected, and
called to be the people of His heavenly kingdom. However, He
came to minister as a Physician, to heal, recover, enliven, and save
them that they might be reconstituted to be His new and heavenly citizens, with whom He could establish His heavenly kingdom on this corrupted earth. (Matt. 9:12, footnote 1)

Today's Reading

Christ as the Son of Man (Jesus), going from Judea to Galilee,
detoured into the city of Sychar, near Jacob's well, to purposely
wait for the thirsty and water-seeking, immoral Samaritan woman (John 4:2-9)—cherishing. The very God who became a man
traveled from Judea to Galilee, and He purposely detoured to a
small city to cherish an immoral woman.

Christ as the Son of God, sent by God as a gift, gave her to
drink the water of life which springs up into eternal life (John
4:10-14)—nourishing. First, He was the Son of Man to cherish
her; then He was the Son of God to give her the living water that
flows into the New Jerusalem, the totality of the eternal life.

Christ as the Son of Man would not condemn the sinful

woman (John 8:11b)—cherishing. This sinful woman was accused by the scribes and Pharisees, but eventually they were condemned by Christ....The Lord said to the woman, "Has no one condemned you?" She said, "No one, Lord." Then He said, "Neither do I condemn you" (vv. 10-11). This is cherishing. None of the scribes and Pharisees could say that he was without sin. The Son of Man is the unique One without sin, so He was the only one qualified to condemn the sinful woman, but He would not do it. He came not to condemn the lost but to save them.

Christ as the Son of God (the very "I Am") would free her from sin so that she could sin no more (John 8:11b, 24, 36)—nourishing. According to Exodus 3:14-15, the great "I Am" is the name of Jehovah. *Jehovah* means "I Am That I Am." The Lord told the Pharisees that if they would not believe in Him as the I Am, they would die in their sins (John 8:24). In other words, they would never be freed from their sins but would remain in their sins until they would die in them. The sinful woman, no doubt, believed in the Lord Jesus, taking Him as the very I Am, to be freed from her sins [v. 36]....Only the Son of God in His divinity can enable us to sin no more. As the Son of Man, He will not condemn us but forgive us, and as the Son of God, He will free us from sinning.

Christ as the Son of Man went to Jericho, passed by the tree from which Zaccheus was expecting to see Him, and looked up and said to him, "Zaccheus, hurry and come down, for today I must stay in your house," in order to cherish him that He might nourish him with His salvation (Luke 19:1-10).

When His disciples rejected people bringing their children to Him, He stopped their preventing and asked them to bring the children to Him, and He cherished the parents by laying His hands on their children (Matt. 19:13-15). The disciples' preventing surely offended the parents. Quite often we are preventing people instead of cherishing people. The Lord stopped the disciples' preventing. (*The Vital Groups,* pp. 84-86, 99, 98)

Further Reading: The Vital Groups, msg. 10

Enlightenment and inspiration: _____

_____

_____

_____

Morning Nourishment

John   Then when they had eaten breakfast, Jesus said to
21:15-16 Simon Peter, Simon, *son* of John, do you love Me more
        than these? He said to Him, Yes, Lord, You know that
        I love You. He said to him, Feed My lambs. He said to
        him again a second time, Simon, *son* of John, do you
        love Me? He said to Him, Yes, Lord, You know that
        I love You. He said to him, Shepherd My sheep.

A proof that our vital group is prevailing is that we love people without any discrimination. Some Christian co-workers may feel that we should let certain persons suffer eternal perdition. They may say that they would not love certain persons, such as bank robbers. But while Christ was being crucified on the cross, two robbers were crucified with Him (Matt. 27:38). One of them said, "Jesus, remember me when You come into Your kingdom" (Luke 23:42). Jesus said to him, "Truly I say to you, Today you shall be with Me in Paradise" (v. 43). The first one saved by Christ through His crucifixion was not a gentleman, but a criminal, a robber, sentenced to death. This is very meaningful. (*The Vital Groups*, p. 71)

Today's Reading

John 21 is the completion and consummation of the Gospel of John...showing that Christ's heavenly ministry and the apostles' ministry on the earth cooperate together to carry out God's New Testament economy.

When the Lord stayed with His disciples after His resurrection and before His ascension, in one of His appearings, He commissioned Peter to feed His lambs and shepherd His sheep in His absence, while He is in the heavens (John 21:15-17)....To shepherd is to take all-inclusive tender care of the flock....This is to incorporate the apostolic ministry with Christ's heavenly ministry to take care of God's flock, which is the church that issues in the Body of Christ. (*Crystallization-study of the Gospel of John*, pp. 130-131)

Christ is the best model of cherishing and nourishing as seen in Revelation 1. In verses 12 and 13 John said, "I turned to see the voice that spoke with me; and when I turned, I saw seven golden lampstands, and in the midst of the lampstands One like the Son of Man, clothed with a garment reaching to the feet, and girded about at the breasts with a golden girdle."...This garment is the priestly robe (Exo. 28:33-35), which shows that Christ is our great High Priest.

To be girded at the loins is to be strengthened for the work. Christ has finished His divine work in producing the churches. Now by His love He is caring for the churches which He has produced. This is why He is girded at the breasts. Today Christ is our High Priest taking care of His churches established by His labor,...wearing a golden girdle on His breasts...signifying Christ's divinity becoming His energy....His divine energy is exercised by and with His love to nourish the churches.

Christ takes care of the churches as the lampstands in His humanity as "the Son of Man" to cherish them (Rev. 1:13a). Christ as our High Priest takes care of the churches He has established first in His humanity to cherish the churches, to make the churches happy, pleasant, and comfortable.

He does this by dressing the lamps of the lampstand...to make them proper [Exo. 30:7]....Christ cares for the lampstands by trimming the wicks of the lamps of the lampstand, just as the priest did according to the type in the Old Testament (Exo. 25:38). When the wick was burned out, it became charred and black, so the priest had to come to cut off the black part of the wick. This is what it means to snuff the wick so that the lamp may shine better. The charred part of the wick, the snuff, signifies things that are not according to God's purpose which need to be cut off, such as our flesh, our natural man, our self, and our old creation. All the lampstands are organic. They are living lampstands. Since each church is a living lampstand, each church has much feeling. A church with charred wicks will not feel comfortable. (*The Vital Groups,* pp. 105-106)

Further Reading: The Vital Groups, msgs. 8, 11; *Crystallization-study of the Gospel of John,* msgs. 7, 13; *The Secret of God's Organic Salvation—"the Spirit Himself with Our Spirit",* ch. 2

Enlightenment and inspiration: _____

_____

_____

_____

Morning Nourishment

Acts Take heed to yourselves and to all the flock, among
20:28 whom the Holy Spirit has placed you as overseers
to shepherd the church of God...
2 Cor. You are our letter, inscribed in our hearts, known and
3:2-3 read by all men, since you are being manifested that
you are a letter of Christ ministered by us, inscribed
not with ink but with the Spirit of the living God...

We need to contact and take care of others, sinners and believers, as the apostle Paul, the top apostle, did in contacting people and taking care of people's need (2 Cor. 1:23—2:14). In 2 Corinthians 11:28-29 Paul said, "Apart from the things which have not been mentioned, there is this: the crowd of cares pressing upon me daily, the anxious concern for all the churches. Who is weak, and I am not weak? Who is stumbled, and I myself do not burn?" This unveils the care of a proper shepherd. (*The Vital Groups*, p. 61)

Today's Reading

Our attitude may be that everyone is weak but we are not weak....In 1 Corinthians 9:22 Paul said, "To the weak I became weak that I might gain the weak." This means that we should come down to the weak one's level....This is the way to shepherd people by visiting them. Paul also said, "Who is stumbled, and I myself do not burn?" [2 Cor. 11:29b]. This is to burn in sorrow and indignation over the cause of the stumbling of all the fallen ones. This shows the pattern of Paul as a good shepherd, taking care of God's flock. (*The Vital Groups*, p. 61)

In Paul's talk with the elders in Ephesus in Acts 20, Paul said that he taught them "publicly and from house to house" (v. 20)....In addition to all of his labor, he still visited the homes of the saints, from house to house. He did this to perfect the saints.

Paul went back again and again to every home of the saints, exhorting them and advising them with tears. An apostle should speak full of sympathy, with tears. Do you want to be an apostle? Then learn how to weep. In Acts 20:19, Paul said that he served the Lord as a slave with all humility and tears. Then in verse 31 he says that he did not cease admonishing each one of the saints with tears. An apostle tells the dear ones under his shepherding everything concerning God and His counsel with tears. He does not only speak publicly, but he also visits the homes of the saints. (*Further Light concerning the Building Up of the Body of Christ,* pp. 24-26)

Second Corinthians 3:2 speaks of the apostles' hearts, whereas verse 3, the hearts of the believers at Corinth. The one kind of letter is inscribed both in the hearts of the apostles and in the hearts of the believers.

According to verse 3, the letter of Christ is "inscribed not with ink but with the Spirit of the living God." The Spirit of the living God, who is the living God Himself, is...the very element, like the ink, with which the apostles minister Christ as the content for the writing of living letters that convey Christ. The writer of this letter is not the Spirit of God; the writer is the apostles....This means that the Spirit of the living God is the element with which the letter is written. This is a very crucial matter.

The one writing produced two original copies. This kind of writing does not take place, however, during the course of superficial preaching, [which]...does not produce letters. But the proper, adequate ministry always writes something of Christ both in the hearts of those receiving the ministry and in the heart of the one ministering.

This was the reason the apostles could assure the Corinthians that they would never forget them, for the believers had been written in their hearts. Wherever the apostles went, they carried the believers with them by having them written in their hearts. This matter is very subjective and experiential. It goes beyond being attached together, for it involves two hearts becoming one. (*Life-study of 2 Corinthians,* pp. 48-49, 51)

Further Reading: The Vital Groups, msg. 7; *Further Light concerning the Building Up of the Body of Christ,* ch. 2; *Life-study of 2 Corinthians,* msg. 6

Enlightenment and inspiration: _____

_____

_____

_____

Morning Nourishment

2 Cor. But I, I will most gladly spend and be utterly spent
12:15 on behalf of your souls. If I love you more abundantly, am I loved less?

Phil. But even if I am being poured out as a drink offer-
2:17 ing upon the sacrifice and service of your faith, I
rejoice, and I rejoice together with you all.

The drink offering was in addition to the basic offerings
revealed in Leviticus 1—6 (Num. 15:1-10; 28:7-10)....The drink
offering is a type of Christ as enjoyed by the offerer. Christ as
the heavenly wine fills the offerer and even causes him to
become wine to God. The apostle Paul became such a drink
offering (2 Tim. 4:6) by enjoying Christ in this way, so that he
could be poured out as a sacrifice to God upon the believers'
faith through the shedding of his blood. (Phil. 2:17, footnote 1)

Today's Reading

The end of 1 Corinthians 12 reveals that love is the most excellent way (v. 31b). How can one be an elder? Love is the most
excellent way. How can one be a co-worker? Love is the most excellent way. How do we shepherd people? Love is the most excellent way. Love is the most excellent way for us to prophesy and to
teach others. Love is the most excellent way for us to be anything
or do anything.

Love prevails. We should love everybody, even our enemies. If
the co-workers and elders do not love the bad ones, eventually they
will have nothing to do. We must be perfect as our Father is perfect
(Matt. 5:48) by loving the evil ones and the good ones without any
discrimination. We must be perfect as our Father because we are
His sons, His species....How can we be a co-worker and an elder? It
is by love in every way. We must love any kind of person. The Lord
Jesus said that He came to be a Physician, not for the healthy ones,
but for the sick ones. The Lord said, "Those who are strong have no
need of a physician, but those who are ill" (Matt. 9:12).

The church is not a police station to arrest people or a law
court to judge people but a home to raise up the believers.

Parents know that the worse their children are, the more they need their raising up. If our children were angels, they would not need our parenting to raise them up. The church is a loving home to raise up the children. The church is also a hospital to heal and to recover the sick ones. Finally, the church is a school to teach and edify the unlearned ones who do not have much understanding. Because the church is a home, a hospital, and a school, the co-workers and elders should be one with the Lord to raise up, to heal, to recover, and to teach others in love.

Some of the churches, however, are police stations to arrest the sinful ones and law courts to judge them. Paul's attitude was different. He said, "Who is weak, and I am not weak?" (2 Cor. 11:29a). When the scribes and Pharisees brought an adulterous woman to the Lord, He said to them, "He who is without sin among you, let him be the first to throw a stone at her" (John 8:7). After all of them left, the Lord asked the sinful woman, "Woman, where are they? Has no one condemned you?" She said, "No one, Lord." Then Jesus said, "Neither do I condemn you" (vv. 10-11). Who is without sin? Who is perfect? Paul said, "To the weak I became weak that I might gain the weak" (1 Cor. 9:22). This is love. We should not consider that others are weak but we are not. This is not love. Love covers and builds up, so love is the most excellent way for us to be anything and to do anything for the building up of the Body of Christ.

I hope that there will be a genuine revival among us by our receiving this burden of shepherding. If all the churches receive this teaching to participate in Christ's wonderful shepherding, there will be a big revival in the recovery. In the past we did much speaking and teaching with very little shepherding. Shepherding and teaching should be like two feet for our move with the Lord. Our shepherding should always be with teaching, and our teaching should always be with shepherding. (*The Vital Groups*, pp. 74-75, 40)

Further Reading: Life-study of 2 Corinthians, msg. 44; *The All-inclusive Christ*, chs. 5-6

Enlightenment and inspiration: _____

_____

_____

_____

Hymns, #922

1 To the lost world minister Christ,
     Not just by word, but by life,
  Imparting Christ by living deeds
     To the poor souls living in strife.

    To the lost world minister Christ,
    By daily walk making Him known;
    Imparting Christ by whom you live,
    Share with all men what you own.

2 To the lost world minister Christ,
     The precious One you possess,
  Imparting Christ to those you love
     As all their gain and success.

3 To the lost world minister Christ,
     The very Christ you enjoy,
  Imparting Christ to all your friends
     As all their boast and their joy.

4 To the lost world minister Christ,
     Who is your life and your all,
  Imparting Christ to all you meet,
     All fallen ones, great or small.

*Composition for prophecy with main point and
sub-points:* _____

_____
_____
_____
_____
_____
_____
_____
_____
_____
_____
_____
_____
_____
_____
_____
_____
_____
_____
_____
_____
_____
_____
_____
_____
_____
_____
_____
_____
_____
_____
_____
_____

Shepherding according to God
(2)
Becoming One with God,
Being Constituted with God,
Living God, Expressing God,
Representing God,
and Ministering God
to Shepherd according to God

Scripture Reading: John 21:15-17; Heb. 13:20-21; 1 Pet. 5:2; 1 Cor. 6:17; 2 Cor. 13:14

Day 1
I. **The Lord Jesus incorporated the apostolic ministry with His heavenly ministry in shepherding God's flock, which is the church (Heb. 8:1; 13:20-21; John 21:15-17):**
   A. In His heavenly ministry the Lord Jesus continues the shepherding that He began in His earthly ministry (10:11, 14-16; Heb. 13:20-21).
   B. Regarding shepherding, the apostolic ministry cooperates with Christ's heavenly ministry (1 Pet. 2:25; 5:2-4; John 21:15-17).

II. **In 1 Peter 5:2 the apostle Peter speaks about shepherding according to God:**
   A. To shepherd according to God is to shepherd according to God's nature, desire, way, and glory, not according to our preference, interest, purpose, and disposition (2 Cor. 4:2, 5-6).

Day 2
   B. To shepherd according to God is to shepherd according to what God is in His attributes (1 John 1:5; 4:8; Luke 6:36).

III. **In order to shepherd according to God, we need to become one with God, be constituted with God, live God, express God, represent God, and minister God:**
   A. If we would shepherd according to God, we need to become one with God (John 14:20; 1 Cor. 6:17):
      1. The basic principle of the Bible is that in His economy God is making Himself one with

Day 3

Day 4

man and man one with Him (John 15:4;
1 Cor. 6:17).

2. God desires that the divine life and the
human life be joined together to become one
life that has one living (John 6:57; Gal. 2:20).

3. In 1 Corinthians 7 we see the principle of being one with the Lord in all circumstances,
situations, and conditions (vv. 17, 24).

B. Shepherding according to God requires that we be
constituted with God (Eph. 3:17a; Col. 3:10-11):

1. God desires to dispense Himself into our
being so that our being may be constituted
with His being to be one constitution with
His being (Eph. 3:17a; 4:4-6).

2. As the Divine Being, God infuses us with
His element, causing us to be the same as
He is in life and nature but not in the God-
head (2 Cor. 13:14).

C. Only those who live God can shepherd according
to God (Phil. 1:21a):

1. God's economy is to work Himself into us so
that we may receive Him as our life and life
supply in order to live Him (John 11:25;
6:48, 57).

2. We are participating in the divine life and
the divine nature so that we can live God in
our humanity (Gal. 2:20).

3. Our daily life should actually be God Himself and thus be a life of living God; to walk
in a manner worthy of God is to live God,
that is, to express God in our daily living
(1 Thes. 2:12; 1 Cor. 10:31).

D. God's intention in His economy is to dispense Himself into us as our life and nature, making us the
same as He is in life and nature to express Him
(Eph. 3:16-21; 1 John 5:11-12; Col. 3:4; 2 Pet. 1:4):

1. God's eternal purpose is to work Himself into us as our life so that we may express Him
(Gen. 1:26; Eph. 1:11; 3:11; 2 Tim. 1:9).

2. The human virtues that are produced in us through our eating, digesting, and assimilating God with His attributes become the expression of God (Eph. 4:1-3).

3. God's desire is that we would be one with Him and live Him for His corporate expression (1 Cor. 6:17; Phil. 1:21a; Eph. 1:22-23; 4:16).

Day 5

E. As those who would shepherd according to God, we need to represent God and function as the acting God:

1. Jehovah made Moses "God to Pharaoh"; in Moses, God had one to represent Him and to execute His will (Exo. 7:1; 3:16-18; 5:1).

2. As the representative of God, Samuel was the acting God (1 Sam. 1:11; 2:35; 7:3; 8:22):

    a. Samuel could be the acting God because his being and God's heart were one (2:35).

    b. Samuel's living and working were for carrying out whatever was in God's heart.

3. In his ministry Elisha the prophet, as the man of God, behaved himself as God's representative, as the acting God; today we, the believers in Christ, can be the same (2 Kings 4:9; 1 Tim. 6:11).

4. As an ambassador of Christ, one who represented God, Paul was the acting God (2 Cor. 1:3-4, 12, 15-16; 2:10; 10:11; 11:2).

Day 6

F. To shepherd according to God is to minister God to others (13:14):

1. Our work in the Lord's recovery today is to minister the processed God to people (Eph. 3:16-17a; 2 Cor. 3:9; 4:1, 5; 13:14).

2. The Triune God is embodied in Christ and realized as the consummated Spirit; this is the God whom we worship, proclaim, and minister to others (Col. 2:9; 1 Cor. 15:45; 2 Cor. 1:3-4; 13:14).

3. Those who minister the word should supply the saints with God and reality, not mere

doctrine (2 Tim. 2:2, 15; 4:2-3, 5).

4. How much we can minister God to others depends on our being broken by God for the outflow of life (2 Cor. 4:10-12, 16; Heb. 4:12).

5. If we would minister God to one another, we need to speak words of grace, truth, spirit, and life, ministering the processed God who has been wrought into our being (Eph. 3:16-17a; 4:25, 29; John 6:63).

6. We need to feed the saints with God so that they may receive the supply of life with full enjoyment and satisfaction for the building up of the Body of Christ (Matt. 24:45-46; Heb. 5:12-14; Eph. 4:16).

Morning Nourishment

John   He said to him again a second time, Simon, *son* of
21:16 John, do you love Me? He said to Him, Yes, Lord,
       You know that I love You. He said to him, Shepherd
       My sheep.
1 Pet. Shepherd the flock of God among you, overseeing not
  5:2   under compulsion but willingly, according to God;
        not by seeking gain through base means but eagerly.

The Lord unveiled to the disciples that He was the good Shepherd who came that the sheep might have life abundantly and that He had other sheep (the Gentiles) which He must lead to join with them (the Jewish believers) to be one flock (one church) under one Shepherd....The Lord's shepherding was firstly in His earthly ministry (Matt. 9:36). The Lord saw the Israelites as sheep harassed by their leaders; they were cast away like sheep not having a shepherd. The Lord as the Shepherd of God's elect prayed, and God told His sent One to appoint twelve apostles that they might take care of the sheep of God (Matt. 10:1-6)....The Lord's shepherding is secondly in His heavenly ministry (1 Pet. 5:4) to take care of the church of God, issuing in His Body. When He was on the earth, He was shepherding. After His resurrection and ascension to the heavens, He is still shepherding. (*Crystallization-study of the Gospel of John,* pp. 130-131)

Today's Reading

When the Lord stayed with His disciples after His resurrection and before His ascension, in one of His appearings, He commissioned Peter to feed His lambs and shepherd His sheep in His absence, while He is in the heavens (John 21:15-17). Shepherding implies feeding, but it includes much more than feeding. To shepherd is to take all-inclusive tender care of the flock.... This is to incorporate the apostolic ministry with Christ's heavenly ministry to take care of God's flock, which is the church that issues in the Body of Christ.

Christ's shepherding of His flock includes His caring for their outward things and also their inner being, their souls. He takes care of the things concerning their souls by overseeing their souls. Christ indwells us to be our life and everything, but He is also overseeing, observing, the condition and situation of our inner being. He shepherds us by caring for the welfare of our inner being and by exercising His oversight over the condition of our soul, our real person....Peter exhorted the elders to shepherd the flock of God among them so that when the Chief Shepherd is manifested, they, the faithful elders, will receive the unfading crown of glory (1 Pet. 5:1-4)....Peter's word indicates that the heavenly ministry of Christ is mainly to shepherd the church of God as His flock which issues in His Body....The main purpose and goal of the apostolic ministry incorporated with Christ's heavenly ministry are to build up the Body of Christ which will consummate the New Jerusalem for the accomplishment of the eternal economy of God. (*Crystallization-study of the Gospel of John*, pp. 131-133)

Through their experience of the dispensing of the Divine Trinity, the believers should shepherd the saints as the flock of God according to God, that is, according to God's nature, desire, way, and glory. In Acts 20:28 Paul reminded the elders in Ephesus to shepherd the church of God. The main responsibility of the elders as overseers is not to rule over the flock but to shepherd the flock, to take all-inclusive tender care of the flock, the church of God. Shepherding the flock of God requires suffering for the Body of Christ as Christ suffered (Col. 1:24). This kind of shepherding enables the elders to be rewarded with the unfading crown of glory (1 Pet. 5:4).

To shepherd according to God [v. 2] means to shepherd according to God's nature, desire, way, and glory, not according to man's preference, interest, and purpose. The elders should not shepherd the flock according to their own opinion, concepts, or likes and dislikes. Instead, they should shepherd the saints as the flock of God according to God's choice, desire, intention, and preference. (*Truth Lessons—Level Four,* vol. 3, pp. 20-21)

Further Reading: Crystallization-study of the Gospel of John, msg. 13; *The Vital Groups,* msg. 6

Enlightenment and inspiration: _____

_____

_____

_____

Morning Nourishment

John Abide in Me and I in you. As the branch cannot
15:4 bear fruit of itself unless it abides in the vine, so
      neither *can* you unless you abide in Me.
6:57 As the living Father has sent Me and I live because
      of the Father, so he who eats Me, he also shall live
      because of Me.

In his first Epistle, Peter spoke in 2:25 of Christ being the Shepherd and Overseer of our soul, our inner being and real person. Then in 5:1-2 he told the elders that their obligation is to shepherd God's flock according to God. *According to God* means that we must live God. We must have God on hand. We have God in our understanding, in our theology, and in our teaching, but we may not live God when we are shepherding people. When we are one with God, we become God. Then we have God and are God in our shepherding of others. To shepherd according to God is to shepherd according to what God is in His attributes. God is love, light, holiness, and righteousness. *According to God* is at least according to these four attributes of God. We must shepherd the young ones, the weak ones, and the backsliding ones according to these four attributes. Then we will be good shepherds. Without shepherding, there is no way for us to minister life to others. (*The Vital Groups,* pp. 60-61)

Today's Reading

In order to understand the Bible, we must exercise one principle. This principle is that God planned in His economy to make Himself one with man. The basic principle, the main principle, of Christ's birth is that God came to join Himself to man, to be a man, and to be one with man. This is the basic principle of the Bible.

When we read the Bible, we need to keep the principle of God's being one with man. We should keep the principle that the Word of God as the divine revelation shows us that God's main purpose is to make Himself one with man and to make man one with Him. In John 15 the Lord said, "I am the vine; you are the branches....Abide in Me and I in you" (vv. 5, 4). This shows us that God and the believers in Christ are one. We and God were once separate, but one day we, the wild branches, were grafted into Him in Christ (Rom. 11:24). We have been grafted into Christ as the tree, and this grafting has made us one with Him. What is needed now is for us to abide in Him that He may abide in us. Then He and we will be one, having one life, one nature, and one living.

If we see this, we will be fully adjusted in our understanding of the Bible. We need to hold the divine concept in John 15 where the Lord said that He is the vine, that we are His branches, and that we should abide in Him that He may abide in us.

In our understanding of the Bible, we have to pick up the proper principles. The main principle is that God desires to be one with His chosen people. Eventually, the oneness between God and man will be completed, consummated. All of God's chosen people will be consummated to be fully one with God to become the constituents of the holy city, the New Jerusalem. Whenever we come to the Psalms, we need to hold this concept; otherwise, we can be misled. (*Life-study of the Psalms,* pp. 200-201)

We all know that in botany, grafting means to unite two trees. A farmer grafts a branch of a sweet tree into that of a sour tree so that the life of the sweet tree can enter into the sour tree and the life of the sour tree can enter into the sweet tree. Eventually these two lives are joined together to become one life. The fruit produced thereafter is the expression of the sweet tree through the sour tree. To the sour tree, the sweet tree is its life, so it is no longer the sour tree that lives, but it is the sweet tree that lives in it. If the sour tree could speak, it would declare, "As always, even now the sweet tree will be magnified in my body, whether through wind and frost or through rain and snow." This is the life of a Christian. (*The Mystery of the Universe and the Meaning of Human Life,* pp. 27-28)

Further Reading: CWWL, 1975-1976, vol. 1, "Living in the Spirit," chs. 1-3

Enlightenment and inspiration: _____

_____

_____

_____

Morning Nourishment

Col. **And have put on the new man, which is being re-**
3:10-11 **newed unto full knowledge according to the image of**
Him who created him, where there cannot be Greek
and Jew, circumcision and uncircumcision, barbarian,
Scythian, slave, free man, but Christ is all and in all.

Paul's spirit was absolutely one with God. Paul was not willing to change anything or to initiate anything. This was the reason he could tell the Corinthians not to change their status as far as marriage was concerned. Those who were married when called by the Lord should remain married. This principle applies even to marriage with an unbeliever. The married believer should not initiate any change. On the contrary, the entire matter should be left with God. Whether the unbelieving party remains or leaves, the believing one should take the situation from the Lord. Everything depends on God and on the situations, circumstances, and conditions arranged by Him. (*Life-study of 1 Corinthians,* p. 372)

Today's Reading

It is important to see this principle of being absolutely one with the Lord in all circumstances, situations, and conditions. If we are mindful of this principle as we read 1 Corinthians 7, we shall see that Paul is utterly one with the Lord and that in his instructions and answers he spontaneously and unconsciously expresses such an absolute spirit. Because Paul had this kind of spirit, he could answer the Corinthians' questions in a clear and absolute way, in a way that would help them also to become one with God in their situation. (*Life-study of 1 Corinthians,* p. 373)

The law of life within us is for God's economy. Without giving us His life as the inner law, God has no way to accomplish His economy. God's economy is to dispense Himself into our being that our being may be constituted with His being to be one constitution with His being. This can be accomplished only by God putting Himself into us as the divine life. Today hardly any Christians pay attention to the divine life as the inner law. (*Life-study of Jeremiah,* p. 179)

We may use other terms to describe God's desire to dispense Himself into us. God wants to water us, feed us, refresh us, and nourish us. These terms indicate that God wants to be our life, life supply, food, drink, and air. He is our food to nourish us; our drink to quench our thirst; our air to refresh us; and our life supply to enrich us. As the Divine Being, He infuses us with His elements, causing us to be the same as He in life and nature.

In His economy God does not improve us outwardly. Instead, He transmits all that He is into us. The difference between outward correction and inward transfusion can be illustrated by the difference between applying makeup and having a healthy complexion because of eating properly. Man's way is to apply makeup. God's way is to transform us metabolically; it is to nourish, refresh, water, enrich, and strengthen us. This is God's economy.... God does not merely teach us; He nourishes us, waters us, and infuses all His riches into our inner being. This is God's way.

There is a great difference between God's economy and the natural human concept. Our concept is that after we are saved we should make up our minds to improve our behavior. Probably every genuine Christian has made such a decision. According to our concept, we need to improve ourselves. Conscious of our weakness, we beg God to help us. However, God does not answer this kind of prayer. The more we pray that He will help us to improve, the less He will do. On the contrary, our behavior may even worsen. The reason for this is that the concept of receiving help from God to improve our behavior is contrary to God's economy. God's economy is to dispense Himself into us and to work Himself into us that we may take Him as our life and life supply in order to live Him. This is not to have an improved human character; it is to live God. According to His economy, God's intention is to impart His element, His substance, and the ingredients of His nature into our being that we may live Him. (*Life-study of Philippians*, pp. 324, 323)

Further Reading: Life-study of Jeremiah, msg. 32; *The God-man Living*, msgs. 8-9

Enlightenment and inspiration: _____

_____

_____

_____

Morning Nourishment

1 Thes.   So that you might walk in a manner worthy of God,
2:12   who calls you into His own kingdom and glory.
Phil.   For to me, to live is Christ...
1:21

Eventually, we Christians should live a life of God and man, the life of a God-man. Today we live as a man, yet we also live as God in His life and in His nature but not in His Godhead. His Godhead is unique. We have His life and His nature, just as the children of a father have their father's life and nature. But none of the children have the fatherhood. Only the father of a family has the fatherhood. In the same way, God is unique and His Godhead is unique. We cannot share in His Godhead, but we do have the divine life and the divine nature. We are participating in this divine life and divine nature so that we can live God, live Christ.

We need to be released from being misled and be brought into the central line of God's economy, which is to live Christ as the embodiment of God by the realization of the Spirit. Today we are here as a man, but we are living the Triune God in our manhood. (*Life-study of the Psalms,* pp. 210-211)

Today's Reading

We have placed a strong emphasis on the fact that, according to 1 Thessalonians 1:1, the church is an entity in God the Father and the Lord Jesus Christ. Now let us go on to consider 2:12: "That you might walk in a manner worthy of God, who calls you into His own kingdom and glory." What does it mean to walk worthily of God? To walk worthily of God is to have a life in the Lord Jesus Christ. First Thessalonians 2:12 is an explanation of 1:1. What does it mean for the church to be in God the Father and the Lord Jesus Christ? For the church to be in God the Father and the Lord Jesus Christ in a practical way is for there to be a company of human beings who walk worthily of God.

What can compare with God? What can match Him? The answer to these questions is that only God Himself can compare with God or match Him. This indicates that to walk worthily of God actually means to live God. Our daily life must actually be God Himself, since only God can be worthy of God, match God, or compare with God. Therefore, in our living we must express God. (*Life-study of 1 Thessalonians*, p. 84)

The Bible is a complete revelation. The content of this revelation is God's eternal purpose. As we have pointed out many times, God's eternal purpose is to work Himself into a corporate man so that He may have a corporate expression in the universe. If we would understand any portion of the Bible in a proper way, we must keep this matter in mind. (*Life-study of Genesis*, p. 813)

The God of whom we have been constituted will express Himself from within us. In what way is the God whom we eat and digest and of whom we are constituted expressed from within us? God is expressed in us by means of His attributes. God is love and light, and He is holy and righteous. When we eat and drink of God, we shall live Him as love, light, holiness, and righteousness. These divine attributes will become our virtues as the expression of God. How can we tell that someone has been eating and digesting God? We can tell this by the expression of God from within him. This expression of God is God's speaking. The human virtues that are produced through assimilating God with His divine attributes become the expression of God, and this expression is actually God's speaking. (*Life-study of 1 John*, p. 29)

God has an economy, and this economy involves a plan with many arrangements. God's aim in His economy is to have a group of human beings who have His life and nature inwardly and His image and likeness outwardly. This group of people is a corporate entity, the Body of Christ, to be one with Him and live Him for His corporate expression. As God is expressed not only by the Body but also through the Body, He is glorified. When He is glorified, His people are also glorified in His glorification. In this way God and man are one in glory. (*Life-study of Jeremiah*, p. 82)

Further Reading: CWWL, 1975-1976, vol. 1, "Living in the Spirit," chs. 4-5; *Life Lessons*, lsn. 34

Enlightenment and inspiration: _____

_____

_____

_____

Morning Nourishment

Exo. ...And you shall come, you and the elders of Israel,
3:18 to the king of Egypt, and you shall say to him, Jehovah, the God of the Hebrews, has met with us; and
now let us go a three days' journey into the wilderness that we may sacrifice to Jehovah our God.

2 Cor. For I am jealous over you with a jealousy of God;
11:2 for I betrothed you to one husband to present *you
as* a pure virgin to Christ.

In Exodus we see both the stubborn Pharaoh and Moses, God's
representative. By Pharaoh God made Himself manifest as the
sovereign God, but in Moses God had one to represent Him and to
execute His will. Praise the Lord that none of us are Pharaoh but
we all are Moses, those who are one with the Lord! In His sover-
eignty and mercy, wherever we go, we go with the Lord, we represent Him, and we execute His will. (*Life-study of Exodus*, p. 246)

Today's Reading

At the end of his ministry,...Samuel had reached the highest
position. We may say that in the whole universe, there was only one
who was above him, and that one was God. We may even say that,
as God's representative, Samuel was the acting God. God intended
to move, to act, yet He needed a representative. Samuel thus became a prophet, a priest, and a judge. He was God's oracle and
God's administration. As such, he was the acting God on earth.

Samuel was faithful to God to do according to what was in
God's heart and mind. His whole being and person, not just his
doing, living, and work, were according to God. Samuel's being
and God's heart were one. For this reason it is not too much to
say that Samuel, a man according to God, was the acting God
on earth. God's mind was Samuel's consideration. He had no
other thought, consideration, or thinking. His living and working were for the carrying out of whatever was in God's heart.
(*Life-study of 1 & 2 Samuel*, pp. 43, 28-29)

In his ministry Elisha the prophet, as the man of God,
behaved himself as God's representative, as the acting God, on

the earth. As believers in Christ, we can be the same. (*Life-study of 1 & 2 Kings,* pp. 93-94)

The apostle Paul was an ambassador of Christ. An ambassador is one who represents the highest authority....The highest authority in this universe is God, and God has given all authority in heaven and on earth to Christ (Matt. 28:18). God has appointed Christ to be the King of kings and the Lord of lords (1 Tim. 6:15; Rev. 17:14). Today Jesus is the Christ, the Lord of all, the highest authority. For this highest authority there is the need of some ambassadors on this earth who are qualified to represent Him. The Lord's ministry is not a matter of merely being a preacher or a teacher but of being one who is authorized with the heavenly authority, representing the highest authority in the whole universe. First, we need to be captured by Christ, and eventually, we need to become a representative of Christ on this earth to deal with the earthly nations as an ambassador.

Many years ago I had a card that said "Bondslave of Christ—Witness Lee." At that time I did not dare to entitle myself an ambassador of Christ, but now I have a fuller realization that we all have to be ambassadors of Christ on this earth. We are not only the captives of Christ. Eventually, we have to be the ambassadors of Christ representing Him on this earth for His interests. We may think that this is something too great, too big. Maybe some of the sisters would think that they are just the weak vessels. They may wonder how they could be the ambassadors of Christ, representing the highest authority on this earth. Regardless of whether we are a brother or a sister, all of us are members of the Body of Christ. The highest authority is Christ as the Head, and we as members of the Body have to be representatives of the Head. As representatives of the Head, we are ambassadors. (*CWWL, 1967,* vol. 2, "An Autobiography of a Person in the Spirit," pp. 171-172)

Further Reading: Life-study of Exodus, msg. 22; *CWWL, 1967,* vol. 2, "An Autobiography of a Person in the Spirit," ch. 6

Enlightenment and inspiration: _____

_____

_____

_____

Morning Nourishment

2 Cor. The grace of the Lord Jesus Christ and the love of God
13:14 and the fellowship of the Holy Spirit be with you all.
John It is the Spirit who gives life; the flesh profits noth-
6:63 ing; the words which I have spoken to you are
spirit and are life.

Our work in the recovery today is to minister God to people.
Yes, we need to save sinners and to feed the saints and perfect
them. The crucial matter, however, is that we minister God to
others. The God whom we minister is not just the building
God—He is also the builded God. If we fail to minister God in
this way, our work will be wood, grass, and stubble (1 Cor. 3:12).
(*Life-study of 1 & 2 Samuel*, pp. 200-201)

Today's Reading

I would ask you to reconsider the work you are doing for the
Lord. Perhaps you have opened up a region or have brought
many people to God. But I ask you this question: How much of
Christ as the embodiment of the Triune God has been wrought
into those whom you have brought to God? If we are sincere and
genuine, we will humble ourselves and confess that not very
much of the Triune God has been wrought into the ones we have
brought to God. Therefore, we need to practice one thing—to
minister the processed Triune God into others so that He may
build Himself into their inner man. In every aspect of our
work—preaching the gospel, feeding the believers, perfecting
the saints—the intrinsic element must be that we minister the
building and builded God to others.

The processed Triune God is embodied in Christ and realized as the consummated Spirit. This is the God whom we worship, preach, and minister to others. Today He is building Himself into His redeemed people in order to produce a house with
Himself as the element and also with something from their
redeemed and uplifted humanity. This house is the church, the
Body of Christ. (*Life-study of 1 & 2 Samuel*, p. 201)

We often say that God is life and that He enters into us to be our life. However, because we do not see this vision, we do not speak concerning this in our messages, nor do we help the saints to see this. Those who minister the word must see that the church needs the supply of life, words of life, not the interpretation of doctrines. The ministry of the word is to supply the saints with God as the Spirit of life. The word that is spoken must be spirit and life. This causes the saints to touch God. This is the urgent need in the churches today. (*The Perfecting of the Saints and the Building Up of the House of God,* p. 82)

We must remember that the outer man constitutes the greatest hindrance to the ministry of the word....No matter how clever a person is, the outer man can never replace the inner man. The inner man will come up with the right thoughts and proper words to flow out only as the outer man is broken and smashed. The outer shell must be broken by God. The more this shell is broken, the more the life in the spirit will be released. (*CWWN,* vol. 54, "The Breaking of the Outer Man and the Release of the Spirit," p. 205)

In the Old Testament, in addition to the ministries of the priests, kings, and prophets, there was another ministry related to God's people, the ministry of the shepherds (Jer. 23:3-4; Ezek. 34:11-31)....In the Bible God likens His people to a flock, and those who pasture God's people are called shepherds. Shepherds are commissioned by God to feed God's flock so that they may receive the supply of life with full enjoyment and satisfaction.... Besides feeding God's people, shepherds take care of God's people so that they may lie down and have rest. Sometimes shepherds seek out, heal, and rescue....As a shepherd, one also should teach God's people and open their understanding with the holy Word of God so that they may know God and obey God....The most crucial responsibility of a shepherd is to lead God's people so that they are not scattered and led astray but obey and keep God's word and are one flock under God's name. (*Truth Lessons—Level Three,* vol. 2, pp. 123-124)

Further Reading: The Vital Groups, msgs. 7-8

Enlightenment and inspiration: _____

_____

_____

_____

Hymns, #863

1   In daily walk and in our meetings too,
    Christ is the center, Christ is everything;
    'Tis not for form nor doctrine good and true,
    But 'tis for Christ alone we're gathering.

2   Christ is the way and Christ the light of life,
    In Him we walk and by Him we are led;
    Christ is the living water and the food;
    Of Him we drink and we with Him are fed.

3   Christ is the truth, 'tis Him we testify,
    Christ is the life, 'tis Him we minister;
    Christ is the Lord, 'tis Him we magnify,
    Christ is the Head, and we exalt Him here.

4   Christ is the All in all to God and man —
    With Him both we and God are satisfied;
    Christ, the reality within the Church —
    By Him are life and numbers multiplied.

5   By all the hymns and prayers we offer here,
    Christ the reality we would express;
    All the activities in fellowship —
    Christ thus in operation manifest.

6   'Tis in His Name we meet, in Spirit act,
    With nothing in our mind to formalize;
    'Tis by His pow'r we pray, in unction praise,
    And with Himself in spirit exercise.

7   All things forgetting, cleaving unto Christ,
    Applying Him until maturity;
    Let us count everything but loss for Him,
    For Him, our All in all, eternally.

*Composition for prophecy with main point and
sub-points:* _____

_____
_____
_____
_____
_____
_____
_____
_____
_____
_____
_____
_____
_____
_____
_____
_____
_____
_____
_____
_____
_____
_____
_____
_____
_____
_____
_____
_____
_____
_____
_____
_____
_____
_____
_____
_____

Reading Schedule for the Recovery Version of the Old Testament with Footnotes

Wk.	Lord's Day	Monday	Tuesday	Wednesday	Thursday	Friday	Saturday
1	Gen. 1:1-5 ☐	1:6-23 ☐	1:24-31 ☐	2:1-9 ☐	2:10-25 ☐	3:1-13 ☐	3:14-24 ☐
2	4:1-26 ☐	5:1-32 ☐	6:1-22 ☐	7:1—8:3 ☐	8:4-22 ☐	9:1-29 ☐	10:1-32 ☐
3	11:1-32 ☐	12:1-20 ☐	13:1-18 ☐	14:1-24 ☐	15:1-21 ☐	16:1-16 ☐	17:1-27 ☐
4	18:1-33 ☐	19:1-38 ☐	20:1-18 ☐	21:1-34 ☐	22:1-24 ☐	23:1—24:27 ☐	24:28-67 ☐
5	25:1-34 ☐	26:1-35 ☐	27:1-46 ☐	28:1-22 ☐	29:1-35 ☐	30:1-43 ☐	31:1-55 ☐
6	32:1-32 ☐	33:1—34:31 ☐	35:1-29 ☐	36:1-43 ☐	37:1-36 ☐	38:1—39:23 ☐	40:1—41:13 ☐
7	41:14-57 ☐	42:1-38 ☐	43:1-34 ☐	44:1-34 ☐	45:1-28 ☐	46:1-34 ☐	47:1-31 ☐
8	48:1-22 ☐	49:1-15 ☐	49:16-33 ☐	50:1-26 ☐	Exo. 1:1-22 ☐	2:1-25 ☐	3:1-22 ☐
9	4:1-31 ☐	5:1-23 ☐	6:1-30 ☐	7:1-25 ☐	8:1-32 ☐	9:1-35 ☐	10:1-29 ☐
10	11:1-10 ☐	12:1-14 ☐	12:15-36 ☐	12:37-51 ☐	13:1-22 ☐	14:1-31 ☐	15:1-27 ☐
11	16:1-36 ☐	17:1-16 ☐	18:1-27 ☐	19:1-25 ☐	20:1-26 ☐	21:1-36 ☐	22:1-31 ☐
12	23:1-33 ☐	24:1-18 ☐	25:1-22 ☐	25:23-40 ☐	26:1-14 ☐	26:15-37 ☐	27:1-21 ☐
13	28:1-21 ☐	28:22-43 ☐	29:1-21 ☐	29:22-46 ☐	30:1-10 ☐	30:11-38 ☐	31:1-17 ☐
14	31:18—32:35 ☐	33:1-23 ☐	34:1-35 ☐	35:1-35 ☐	36:1-38 ☐	37:1-29 ☐	38:1-31 ☐
15	39:1-43 ☐	40:1-38 ☐	Lev. 1:1-17 ☐	2:1-16 ☐	3:1-17 ☐	4:1-35 ☐	5:1-19 ☐
16	6:1-30 ☐	7:1-38 ☐	8:1-36 ☐	9:1-24 ☐	10:1-20 ☐	11:1-47 ☐	12:1-8 ☐
17	13:1-28 ☐	13:29-59 ☐	14:1-18 ☐	14:19-32 ☐	14:33-57 ☐	15:1-33 ☐	16:1-17 ☐
18	16:18-34 ☐	17:1-16 ☐	18:1-30 ☐	19:1-37 ☐	20:1-27 ☐	21:1-24 ☐	22:1-33 ☐
19	23:1-22 ☐	23:23-44 ☐	24:1-23 ☐	25:1-23 ☐	25:24-55 ☐	26:1-24 ☐	26:25-46 ☐
20	27:1-34 ☐	Num. 1:1-54 ☐	2:1-34 ☐	3:1-51 ☐	4:1-49 ☐	5:1-31 ☐	6:1-27 ☐
21	7:1-41 ☐	7:42-88 ☐	7:89—8:26 ☐	9:1-23 ☐	10:1-36 ☐	11:1-35 ☐	12:1—13:33 ☐
22	14:1-45 ☐	15:1-41 ☐	16:1-50 ☐	17:1—18:7 ☐	18:8-32 ☐	19:1-22 ☐	20:1-29 ☐
23	21:1-35 ☐	22:1-41 ☐	23:1-30 ☐	24:1-25 ☐	25:1-18 ☐	26:1-65 ☐	27:1-23 ☐
24	28:1-31 ☐	29:1-40 ☐	30:1—31:24 ☐	31:25-54 ☐	32:1-42 ☐	33:1-56 ☐	34:1-29 ☐
25	35:1-34 ☐	36:1-13 ☐	Deut. 1:1-46 ☐	2:1-37 ☐	3:1-29 ☐	4:1-49 ☐	5:1-33 ☐
26	6:1—7:26 ☐	8:1-20 ☐	9:1-29 ☐	10:1-22 ☐	11:1-32 ☐	12:1-32 ☐	13:1—14:21 ☐

Reading Schedule for the Recovery Version of the Old Testament with Footnotes

Wk.	Lord's Day	Monday	Tuesday	Wednesday	Thursday	Friday	Saturday
27	14:22—15:23 □	16:1-22 □	17:1—18:8 □	18:9—19:21 □	20:1—21:17 □	21:18—22:30 □	23:1-25 □
28	24:1-22 □	25:1-19 □	26:1-19 □	27:1-26 □	28:1-68 □	29:1-29 □	30:1—31:29 □
29	31:30—32:52 □	33:1-29 □	34:1-12 □	Josh. 1:1-18 □	2:1-24 □	3:1-17 □	4:1-24 □
30	5:1-15 □	6:1-27 □	7:1-26 □	8:1-35 □	9:1-27 □	10:1-43 □	11:1—12:24 □
31	13:1-33 □	14:1—15:63 □	16:1—18:28 □	19:1-51 □	20:1—21:45 □	22:1-34 □	23:1—24:33 □
32	Judg. 1:1-36 □	2:1-23 □	3:1-31 □	4:1-24 □	5:1-31 □	6:1-40 □	7:1-25 □
33	8:1-35 □	9:1-57 □	10:1—11:40 □	12:1—13:25 □	14:1—15:20 □	16:1-31 □	17:1—18:31 □
34	19:1-30 □	20:1-48 □	21:1-25 □	Ruth 1:1-22 □	2:1-23 □	3:1-18 □	4:1-22 □
35	1 Sam. 1:1-28 □	2:1-36 □	3:1—4:22 □	5:1—6:21 □	7:1—8:22 □	9:1-27 □	10:1—11:15 □
36	12:1—13:23 □	14:1-52 □	15:1-35 □	16:1-23 □	17:1-58 □	18:1-30 □	19:1-24 □
37	20:1-42 □	21:1—22:23 □	23:1—24:22 □	25:1-44 □	26:1-25 □	27:1—28:25 □	29:1—30:31 □
38	31:1-13 □	2 Sam. 1:1-27 □	2:1-32 □	3:1-39 □	4:1—5:25 □	6:1-23 □	7:1-29 □
39	8:1—9:13 □	10:1—11:27 □	12:1-31 □	13:1-39 □	14:1-33 □	15:1—16:23 □	17:1—18:33 □
40	19:1-43 □	20:1—21:22 □	22:1-51 □	23:1-39 □	24:1-25 □	1 Kings 1:1-19 □	1:20-53 □
41	2:1-46 □	3:1-23 □	4:1-34 □	5:1—6:38 □	7:1-22 □	7:23-51 □	8:1-36 □
42	8:37-66 □	9:1-28 □	10:1-29 □	11:1-43 □	12:1-33 □	13:1-34 □	14:1-31 □
43	15:1-34 □	16:1—17:24 □	18:1-46 □	19:1-21 □	20:1-43 □	21:1—22:53 □	2 Kings 1:1-18 □
44	2:1—3:27 □	4:1-44 □	5:1—6:33 □	7:1-20 □	8:1-29 □	9:1-37 □	10:1-36 □
45	11:1—12:21 □	13:1—14:29 □	15:1-38 □	16:1-20 □	17:1-41 □	18:1-37 □	19:1-37 □
46	20:1—21:26 □	22:1-20 □	23:1-37 □	24:1—25:30 □	1 Chron. 1:1-54 □	2:1—3:24 □	4:1—5:26 □
47	6:1-81 □	7:1-40 □	8:1-40 □	9:1-44 □	10:1—11:47 □	12:1-40 □	13:1—14:17 □
48	15:1—16:43 □	17:1-27 □	18:1—19:19 □	20:1—21:30 □	22:1—23:32 □	24:1—25:31 □	26:1-32 □
49	27:1-34 □	28:1—29:30 □	2 Chron. 1:1-17 □	2:1—3:17 □	4:1—5:14 □	6:1-42 □	7:1—8:18 □
50	9:1—10:19 □	11:1—12:16 □	13:1—15:19 □	16:1—17:19 □	18:1—19:11 □	20:1-37 □	21:1—22:12 □
51	23:1—24:27 □	25:1—26:23 □	27:1—28:27 □	29:1-36 □	30:1—31:21 □	32:1-33 □	33:1—34:33 □
52	35:1—36:23 □	Ezra 1:1-11 □	2:1-70 □	3:1—4:24 □	5:1—6:22 □	7:1-28 □	8:1-36 □

Reading Schedule for the Recovery Version of the Old Testament with Footnotes

Wk.	Lord's Day	Monday	Tuesday	Wednesday	Thursday	Friday	Saturday
53	9:1—10:44 ☐	Neh. 1:1-11 ☐	2:1—3:32 ☐	4:1—5:19 ☐	6:1-19 ☐	7:1-73 ☐	8:1-18 ☐
54	9:1-20 ☐	9:21-38 ☐	10:1—11:36 ☐	12:1-47 ☐	13:1-31 ☐	Esth. 1:1-22 ☐	2:1—3:15 ☐
55	4:1—5:14 ☐	6:1—7:10 ☐	8:1-17 ☐	9:1—10:3 ☐	Job 1:1-22 ☐	2:1—3:26 ☐	4:1—5:27 ☐
56	6:1—7:21 ☐	8:1—9:35 ☐	10:1—11:20 ☐	12:1—13:28 ☐	14:1—15:35 ☐	16:1—17:16 ☐	18:1—19:29 ☐
57	20:1—21:34 ☐	22:1—23:17 ☐	24:1—25:6 ☐	26:1—27:23 ☐	28:1—29:25 ☐	30:1—31:40 ☐	32:1—33:33 ☐
58	34:1—35:16 ☐	36:1-33 ☐	37:1-24 ☐	38:1-41 ☐	39:1-30 ☐	40:1-24 ☐	41:1-34 ☐
59	42:1-17 ☐	Psa. 1:1-6 ☐	2:1—3:8 ☐	4:1—6:10 ☐	7:1—8:9 ☐	9:1—10:18 ☐	11:1—15:5 ☐
60	16:1—17:15 ☐	18:1-50 ☐	19:1—21:13 ☐	22:1-31 ☐	23:1—24:10 ☐	25:1—27:14 ☐	28:1—30:12 ☐
61	31:1—32:11 ☐	33:1—34:22 ☐	35:1—36:12 ☐	37:1-40 ☐	38:1—39:13 ☐	40:1—41:13 ☐	42:1—43:5 ☐
62	44:1-26 ☐	45:1-17 ☐	46:1—48:14 ☐	49:1—50:23 ☐	51:1—52:9 ☐	53:1—55:23 ☐	56:1—58:11 ☐
63	59:1—61:8 ☐	62:1—64:10 ☐	65:1—67:7 ☐	68:1-35 ☐	69:1—70:5 ☐	71:1—72:20 ☐	73:1—74:23 ☐
64	75:1—77:20 ☐	78:1-72 ☐	79:1—81:16 ☐	82:1—84:12 ☐	85:1—87:7 ☐	88:1—89:52 ☐	90:1—91:16 ☐
65	92:1—94:23 ☐	95:1—97:12 ☐	98:1—101:8 ☐	102:1—103:22 ☐	104:1—105:45 ☐	106:1-48 ☐	107:1-43 ☐
66	108:1—109:31 ☐	110:1—112:10 ☐	113:1—115:18 ☐	116:1—118:29 ☐	119:1-32 ☐	119:33-72 ☐	119:73-120 ☐
67	119:121-176 ☐	120:1—124:8 ☐	125:1—128:6 ☐	129:1—132:18 ☐	133:1—135:21 ☐	136:1—138:8 ☐	139:1—140:13 ☐
68	141:1—144:15 ☐	145:1—147:20 ☐	148:1—150:6 ☐	Prov. 1:1-33 ☐	2:1—3:35 ☐	4:1—5:23 ☐	6:1-35 ☐
69	7:1—8:36 ☐	9:1—10:32 ☐	11:1—12:28 ☐	13:1—14:35 ☐	15:1-33 ☐	16:1-33 ☐	17:1-28 ☐
70	18:1-24 ☐	19:1—20:30 ☐	21:1—22:29 ☐	23:1-35 ☐	24:1—25:28 ☐	26:1—27:27 ☐	28:1—29:27 ☐
71	30:1-33 ☐	31:1-31 ☐	Eccl. 1:1-18 ☐	2:1—3:22 ☐	4:1—5:20 ☐	6:1—7:29 ☐	8:1—9:18 ☐
72	10:1—11:10 ☐	12:1-14 ☐	S.S. 1:1-8 ☐	1:9-17 ☐	2:1-17 ☐	3:1-11 ☐	4:1-8 ☐
73	4:9-16 ☐	5:1-16 ☐	6:1-13 ☐	7:1-13 ☐	8:1-14 ☐	Isa. 1:1-11 ☐	1:12-31 ☐
74	2:1-22 ☐	3:1-26 ☐	4:1-6 ☐	5:1-30 ☐	6:1-13 ☐	7:1-25 ☐	8:1-22 ☐
75	9:1-21 ☐	10:1-34 ☐	11:1—12:6 ☐	13:1-22 ☐	14:1-14 ☐	14:15-32 ☐	15:1—16:14 ☐
76	17:1—18:7 ☐	19:1-25 ☐	20:1—21:17 ☐	22:1-25 ☐	23:1-18 ☐	24:1-23 ☐	25:1-12 ☐
77	26:1-21 ☐	27:1-13 ☐	28:1-29 ☐	29:1-24 ☐	30:1-33 ☐	31:1—32:20 ☐	33:1-24 ☐
78	34:1-17 ☐	35:1-10 ☐	36:1-22 ☐	37:1-38 ☐	38:1—39:8 ☐	40:1-31 ☐	41:1-29 ☐

Reading Schedule for the Recovery Version of the Old Testament with Footnotes

Wk.	Lord's Day	Monday	Tuesday	Wednesday	Thursday	Friday	Saturday
79	42:1-25 ☐	43:1-28 ☐	44:1-28 ☐	45:1-25 ☐	46:1-13 ☐	47:1-15 ☐	48:1-22 ☐
80	49:1-13 ☐	49:14-26 ☐	50:1—51:23 ☐	52:1-15 ☐	53:1-12 ☐	54:1-17 ☐	55:1-13 ☐
81	56:1-12 ☐	57:1-21 ☐	58:1-14 ☐	59:1-21 ☐	60:1-22 ☐	61:1-11 ☐	62:1-12 ☐
82	63:1-19 ☐	64:1-12 ☐	65:1-25 ☐	66:1-24 ☐	Jer. 1:1-19 ☐	2:1-19 ☐	2:20-37 ☐
83	3:1-25 ☐	4:1-31 ☐	5:1-31 ☐	6:1-30 ☐	7:1-34 ☐	8:1-22 ☐	9:1-26 ☐
84	10:1-25 ☐	11:1—12:17 ☐	13:1-27 ☐	14:1-22 ☐	15:1-21 ☐	16:1—17:27 ☐	18:1-23 ☐
85	19:1—20:18 ☐	21:1—22:30 ☐	23:1-40 ☐	24:1—25:38 ☐	26:1—27:22 ☐	28:1—29:32 ☐	30:1-24 ☐
86	31:1-23 ☐	31:24-40 ☐	32:1-44 ☐	33:1-26 ☐	34:1-22 ☐	35:1-19 ☐	36:1-32 ☐
87	37:1-21 ☐	38:1-28 ☐	39:1—40:16 ☐	41:1—42:22 ☐	43:1—44:30 ☐	45:1—46:28 ☐	47:1—48:16 ☐
88	48:17-47 ☐	49:1-22 ☐	49:23-39 ☐	50:1-27 ☐	50:28-46 ☐	51:1-27 ☐	51:28-64 ☐
89	52:1-34 ☐	Lam. 1:1-22 ☐	2:1-22 ☐	3:1-39 ☐	3:40-66 ☐	4:1-22 ☐	5:1-22 ☐
90	Ezek. 1:1-14 ☐	1:15-28 ☐	2:1—3:27 ☐	4:1—5:17 ☐	6:1—7:27 ☐	8:1—9:11 ☐	10:1—11:25 ☐
91	12:1—13:23 ☐	14:1—15:8 ☐	16:1-63 ☐	17:1—18:32 ☐	19:1-14 ☐	20:1-49 ☐	21:1-32 ☐
92	22:1-31 ☐	23:1-49 ☐	24:1-27 ☐	25:1—26:21 ☐	27:1-36 ☐	28:1-26 ☐	29:1—30:26 ☐
93	31:1—32:32 ☐	33:1-33 ☐	34:1-31 ☐	35:1—36:21 ☐	36:22-38 ☐	37:1-28 ☐	38:1—39:29 ☐
94	40:1-27 ☐	40:28-49 ☐	41:1-26 ☐	42:1—43:27 ☐	44:1-31 ☐	45:1-25 ☐	46:1-24 ☐
95	47:1-23 ☐	48:1-35 ☐	Dan. 1:1-21 ☐	2:1-30 ☐	2:31-49 ☐	3:1-30 ☐	4:1-37 ☐
96	5:1-31 ☐	6:1-28 ☐	7:1-12 ☐	7:13-28 ☐	8:1-27 ☐	9:1-27 ☐	10:1-21 ☐
97	11:1-22 ☐	11:23-45 ☐	12:1-13 ☐	Hosea 1:1-11 ☐	2:1-23 ☐	3:1—4:19 ☐	5:1-15 ☐
98	6:1-11 ☐	7:1-16 ☐	8:1-14 ☐	9:1-17 ☐	10:1-15 ☐	11:1-12 ☐	12:1-14 ☐
99	13:1—14:9 ☐	Joel 1:1-20 ☐	2:1-16 ☐	2:17-32 ☐	3:1-21 ☐	Amos 1:1-15 ☐	2:1-16 ☐
100	3:1-15 ☐	4:1—5:27 ☐	6:1—7:17 ☐	8:1—9:15 ☐	Obad. 1-21 ☐	Jonah 1:1-17 ☐	2:1—4:11 ☐
101	Micah 1:1-16 ☐	2:1—3:12 ☐	4:1—5:15 ☐	6:1—7:20 ☐	Nahum 1:1-15 ☐	Hab. 1:1-17 ☐	
102	2:1-20 ☐	3:1-19 ☐	Zeph. 1:1-18 ☐	2:1-15 ☐	3:1-20 ☐	Hag. 1:1-15 ☐	2:1-23 ☐
103	Zech. 1:1-21 ☐	2:1-13 ☐	3:1-10 ☐	4:1-14 ☐	5:1—6:15 ☐	7:1—8:23 ☐	9:1-17 ☐
104	10:1—11:17 ☐	12:1—13:9 ☐	14:1-21 ☐	Mal. 1:1-14 ☐	2:1-17 ☐	3:1-18 ☐	4:1-6 ☐

Reading Schedule for the Recovery Version of the New Testament with Footnotes

Wk.	Lord's Day	Monday	Tuesday	Wednesday	Thursday	Friday	Saturday
1	Matt. 1:1-2 ☐	1:3-7 ☐	1:8-17 ☐	1:18-25 ☐	2:1-23 ☐	3:1-6 ☐	3:7-17 ☐
2	4:1-11 ☐	4:12-25 ☐	5:1-4 ☐	5:5-12 ☐	5:13-20 ☐	5:21-26 ☐	5:27-48 ☐
3	6:1-8 ☐	6:9-18 ☐	6:19-34 ☐	7:1-12 ☐	7:13-29 ☐	8:1-13 ☐	8:14-22 ☐
4	8:23-34 ☐	9:1-13 ☐	9:14-17 ☐	9:18-34 ☐	9:35—10:5 ☐	10:6-25 ☐	10:26-42 ☐
5	11:1-15 ☐	11:16-30 ☐	12:1-14 ☐	12:15-32 ☐	12:33-42 ☐	12:43—13:2 ☐	13:3-12 ☐
6	13:13-30 ☐	13:31-43 ☐	13:44-58 ☐	14:1-13 ☐	14:14-21 ☐	14:22-36 ☐	15:1-20 ☐
7	15:21-31 ☐	15:32-39 ☐	16:1-12 ☐	16:13-20 ☐	16:21-28 ☐	17:1-13 ☐	17:14-27 ☐
8	18:1-14 ☐	18:15-22 ☐	18:23-35 ☐	19:1-15 ☐	19:16-30 ☐	20:1-16 ☐	20:17-34 ☐
9	21:1-11 ☐	21:12-22 ☐	21:23-32 ☐	21:33-46 ☐	22:1-22 ☐	22:23-33 ☐	22:34-46 ☐
10	23:1-12 ☐	23:13-39 ☐	24:1-14 ☐	24:15-31 ☐	24:32-51 ☐	25:1-13 ☐	25:14-30 ☐
11	25:31-46 ☐	26:1-16 ☐	26:17-35 ☐	26:36-46 ☐	26:47-64 ☐	26:65-75 ☐	27:1-26 ☐
12	27:27-44 ☐	27:45-56 ☐	27:57—28:15 ☐	28:16-20 ☐	Mark 1:1 ☐	1:2-6 ☐	1:7-13 ☐
13	1:14-28 ☐	1:29-45 ☐	2:1-12 ☐	2:13-28 ☐	3:1-19 ☐	3:20-35 ☐	4:1-25 ☐
14	4:26-41 ☐	5:1-20 ☐	5:21-43 ☐	6:1-29 ☐	6:30-56 ☐	7:1-23 ☐	7:24-37 ☐
15	8:1-26 ☐	8:27—9:1 ☐	9:2-29 ☐	9:30-50 ☐	10:1-16 ☐	10:17-34 ☐	10:35-52 ☐
16	11:1-16 ☐	11:17-33 ☐	12:1-27 ☐	12:28-44 ☐	13:1-13 ☐	13:14-37 ☐	14:1-26 ☐
17	14:27-52 ☐	14:53-72 ☐	15:1-15 ☐	15:16-47 ☐	16:1-8 ☐	16:9-20 ☐	Luke 1:1-4 ☐
18	1:5-25 ☐	1:26-46 ☐	1:47-56 ☐	1:57-80 ☐	2:1-8 ☐	2:9-20 ☐	2:21-39 ☐
19	2:40-52 ☐	3:1-20 ☐	3:21-38 ☐	4:1-13 ☐	4:14-30 ☐	4:31-44 ☐	5:1-26 ☐
20	5:27—6:16 ☐	6:17-38 ☐	6:39-49 ☐	7:1-17 ☐	7:18-23 ☐	7:24-35 ☐	7:36-50 ☐
21	8:1-15 ☐	8:16-25 ☐	8:26-39 ☐	8:40-56 ☐	9:1-17 ☐	9:18-26 ☐	9:27-36 ☐
22	9:37-50 ☐	9:51-62 ☐	10:1-11 ☐	10:12-24 ☐	10:25-37 ☐	10:38-42 ☐	11:1-13 ☐
23	11:14-26 ☐	11:27-36 ☐	11:37-54 ☐	12:1-12 ☐	12:13-21 ☐	12:22-34 ☐	12:35-48 ☐
24	12:49-59 ☐	13:1-9 ☐	13:10-17 ☐	13:18-30 ☐	13:31—14:6 ☐	14:7-14 ☐	14:15-24 ☐
25	14:25-35 ☐	15:1-10 ☐	15:11-21 ☐	15:22-32 ☐	16:1-13 ☐	16:14-22 ☐	16:23-31 ☐
26	17:1-19 ☐	17:20-37 ☐	18:1-14 ☐	18:15-30 ☐	18:31-43 ☐	19:1-10 ☐	19:11-27 ☐

Reading Schedule for the Recovery Version of the New Testament with Footnotes

Wk.	Lord's Day	Monday	Tuesday	Wednesday	Thursday	Friday	Saturday
27	Luke 19:28-48 ☐	20:1-19 ☐	20:20-38 ☐	20:39—21:4 ☐	21:5-27 ☐	21:28-38 ☐	22:1-20 ☐
28	22:21-38 ☐	22:39-54 ☐	22:55-71 ☐	23:1-43 ☐	23:44-56 ☐	24:1-12 ☐	24:13-35 ☐
29	24:36-53 ☐	John 1:1-13 ☐	1:14-18 ☐	1:19-34 ☐	1:35-51 ☐	2:1-11 ☐	2:12-22 ☐
30	2:23—3:13 ☐	3:14-21 ☐	3:22-36 ☐	4:1-14 ☐	4:15-26 ☐	4:27-42 ☐	4:43-54 ☐
31	5:1-16 ☐	5:17-30 ☐	5:31-47 ☐	6:1-15 ☐	6:16-31 ☐	6:32-51 ☐	6:52-71 ☐
32	7:1-9 ☐	7:10-24 ☐	7:25-36 ☐	7:37-52 ☐	7:53—8:11 ☐	8:12-27 ☐	8:28-44 ☐
33	8:45-59 ☐	9:1-13 ☐	9:14-34 ☐	9:35—10:9 ☐	10:10-30 ☐	10:31—11:4 ☐	11:5-22 ☐
34	11:23-40 ☐	11:41-57 ☐	12:1-11 ☐	12:12-24 ☐	12:25-36 ☐	12:37-50 ☐	13:1-11 ☐
35	13:12-30 ☐	13:31-38 ☐	14:1-6 ☐	14:7-20 ☐	14:21-31 ☐	15:1-11 ☐	15:12-27 ☐
36	16:1-15 ☐	16:16-33 ☐	17:1-5 ☐	17:6-13 ☐	17:14-24 ☐	17:25—18:11 ☐	18:12-27 ☐
37	18:28-40 ☐	19:1-6 ☐	19:17-30 ☐	19:31-42 ☐	20:1-13 ☐	20:14-18 ☐	20:19-22 ☐
38	20:23-31 ☐	21:1-4 ☐	21:15-22 ☐	21:23-25 ☐	Acts 1:1-8 ☐	1:9-14 ☐	1:15-26 ☐
39	2:1-13 ☐	2:14-21 ☐	2:22-36 ☐	2:37-41 ☐	2:42-47 ☐	3:1-18 ☐	3:19—4:22 ☐
40	4:23-37 ☐	5:1-6 ☐	5:17-32 ☐	5:33-42 ☐	6:1—7:1 ☐	7:2-29 ☐	7:30-60 ☐
41	8:1-13 ☐	8:14-25 ☐	8:26-40 ☐	9:1-19 ☐	9:20-43 ☐	10:1-16 ☐	10:17-33 ☐
42	10:34-48 ☐	11:1-18 ☐	11:19-30 ☐	12:1-25 ☐	13:1-12 ☐	13:13-43 ☐	13:44—14:5 ☐
43	14:6-28 ☐	15:1-2 ☐	15:13-34 ☐	15:35—16:5 ☐	16:6-18 ☐	16:19-40 ☐	17:1-18 ☐
44	17:19-34 ☐	18:1-17 ☐	18:18-28 ☐	19:1-20 ☐	19:21-41 ☐	20:1-12 ☐	20:13-38 ☐
45	21:1-14 ☐	21:15-26 ☐	21:27-40 ☐	22:1-21 ☐	22:22-29 ☐	22:30—23:11 ☐	23:12-15 ☐
46	23:16-30 ☐	23:31—24:21 ☐	24:22—25:5 ☐	25:6-27 ☐	26:1-13 ☐	26:14-32 ☐	27:1-26 ☐
47	27:27—28:10 ☐	28:11-22 ☐	28:23-31 ☐	Rom 1:1-2 ☐	1:3-7 ☐	1:8-17 ☐	1:18-25 ☐
48	1:26—2:10 ☐	2:11-29 ☐	3:1-20 ☐	3:21-31 ☐	4:1-12 ☐	4:13-25 ☐	5:1-11 ☐
49	5:12-17 ☐	5:18—6:5 ☐	6:6-11 ☐	6:12-23 ☐	7:1-12 ☐	7:13-25 ☐	8:1-2 ☐
50	8:3-6 ☐	8:7-13 ☐	8:14-25 ☐	8:26-39 ☐	9:1-18 ☐	9:19—10:3 ☐	10:4-15 ☐
51	10:16—11:10 ☐	11:11-22 ☐	11:23-36 ☐	12:1-3 ☐	12:4-21 ☐	13:1-14 ☐	14:1-12 ☐
52	14:13-23 ☐	15:1-13 ☐	15:14-33 ☐	16:1-5 ☐	16:6-24 ☐	16:25-27 ☐	1 Cor. 1:1-4 ☐

Reading Schedule for the Recovery Version of the New Testament with Footnotes

Wk.	Lord's Day	Monday	Tuesday	Wednesday	Thursday	Friday	Saturday
53	1 Cor. 1:5-9 ☐	1:10-17 ☐	1:18-31 ☐	2:1-5 ☐	2:6-10 ☐	2:11-16 ☐	3:1-9 ☐
54	3:10-13 ☐	3:14-23 ☐	4:1-9 ☐	4:10-21 ☐	5:1-13 ☐	6:1-11 ☐	6:12-20 ☐
55	7:1-16 ☐	7:17-24 ☐	7:25-40 ☐	8:1-13 ☐	9:1-15 ☐	9:16-27 ☐	10:1-4 ☐
56	10:5-13 ☐	10:14-33 ☐	11:1-6 ☐	11:7-16 ☐	11:17-26 ☐	11:27-34 ☐	12:1-11 ☐
57	12:12-22 ☐	12:23-31 ☐	13:1-13 ☐	14:1-12 ☐	14:13-25 ☐	14:26-33 ☐	14:34-40 ☐
58	15:1-19 ☐	15:20-28 ☐	15:29-34 ☐	15:35-49 ☐	15:50-58 ☐	16:1-9 ☐	16:10-24 ☐
59	2 Cor. 1:1-4 ☐	1:5-14 ☐	1:15-22 ☐	1:23—2:11 ☐	2:12-17 ☐	3:1-6 ☐	3:7-11 ☐
60	3:12-18 ☐	4:1-6 ☐	4:7-12 ☐	4:13-18 ☐	5:1-8 ☐	5:9-15 ☐	5:16-21 ☐
61	6:1-13 ☐	6:14—7:4 ☐	7:5-16 ☐	8:1-15 ☐	8:16-24 ☐	9:1-15 ☐	10:1-6 ☐
62	10:7-18 ☐	11:1-15 ☐	11:16-33 ☐	12:1-10 ☐	12:11-21 ☐	13:1-10 ☐	13:11-14 ☐
63	Gal. 1:1-5 ☐	1:6-14 ☐	1:15-24 ☐	2:1-13 ☐	2:14-21 ☐	3:1-4 ☐	3:5-14 ☐
64	3:15-22 ☐	3:23-29 ☐	4:1-7 ☐	4:8-20 ☐	4:21-31 ☐	5:1-12 ☐	5:13-21 ☐
65	5:22-26 ☐	6:1-10 ☐	6:11-15 ☐	6:16-18 ☐	Eph. 1:1-3 ☐	1:4-6 ☐	1:7-10 ☐
66	1:11-14 ☐	1:15-18 ☐	1:19-23 ☐	2:1-5 ☐	2:6-10 ☐	2:11-14 ☐	2:15-18 ☐
67	2:19-22 ☐	3:1-7 ☐	3:8-13 ☐	3:14-18 ☐	3:19-21 ☐	4:1-4 ☐	4:5-10 ☐
68	4:11-16 ☐	4:17-24 ☐	4:25-32 ☐	5:1-10 ☐	5:11-21 ☐	5:22-26 ☐	5:27-33 ☐
69	6:1-9 ☐	6:10-14 ☐	6:15-18 ☐	6:19-24 ☐	Phil. 1:1-7 ☐	1:8-18 ☐	1:19-26 ☐
70	1:27—2:4 ☐	2:5-11 ☐	2:12-16 ☐	2:17-30 ☐	3:1-6 ☐	3:7-11 ☐	3:12-16 ☐
71	3:17-21 ☐	4:1-9 ☐	4:10-23 ☐	Col. 1:1-8 ☐	1:9-13 ☐	1:14-23 ☐	1:24-29 ☐
72	2:1-7 ☐	2:8-15 ☐	2:16-23 ☐	3:1-4 ☐	3:5-15 ☐	3:16-25 ☐	4:1-18 ☐
73	1 Thes. 1:1-3 ☐	1:4-10 ☐	2:1-12 ☐	2:13—3:5 ☐	3:6-13 ☐	4:1-10 ☐	4:11—5:11 ☐
74	5:12-28 ☐	2 Thes. 1:1-12 ☐	2:1-17 ☐	3:1-18 ☐	1 Tim. 1:1-2 ☐	1:3-4 ☐	1:5-14 ☐
75	1:15-20 ☐	2:1-7 ☐	2:8-15 ☐	3:1-13 ☐	3:14—4:5 ☐	4:6-16 ☐	5:1-25 ☐
76	6:1-10 ☐	6:11-21 ☐	2 Tim. 1:1-10 ☐	1:11-18 ☐	2:1-15 ☐	2:16-26 ☐	3:1-13 ☐
77	3:14—4:8 ☐	4:9-22 ☐	Titus 1:1-4 ☐	1:5-16 ☐	2:1-15 ☐	3:1-8 ☐	3:9-15 ☐
78	Philem. 1:1-11 ☐	1:12-25 ☐	Heb. 1:1-2 ☐	1:3-5 ☐	1:6-14 ☐	2:1-9 ☐	2:10-18 ☐

Reading Schedule for the Recovery Version of the New Testament with Footnotes

Wk.	Lord's Day	Monday	Tuesday	Wednesday	Thursday	Friday	Saturday
79	Heb. 3:1-6 ☐	3:7-19 ☐	4:1-9 ☐	4:10-13 ☐	4:14-16 ☐	5:1-10 ☐	5:11—6:3 ☐
80	6:4-8 ☐	6:9-20 ☐	7:1-10 ☐	7:11-28 ☐	8:1-6 ☐	8:7-13 ☐	9:1-4 ☐
81	9:5-14 ☐	9:15-28 ☐	10:1-18 ☐	10:19-28 ☐	10:29-39 ☐	11:1-6 ☐	11:7-19 ☐
82	11:20-31 ☐	11:32-40 ☐	12:1-2 ☐	12:3-13 ☐	12:14-17 ☐	12:18-26 ☐	12:27-29 ☐
83	13:1-7 ☐	13:8-12 ☐	13:13-15 ☐	13:16-25 ☐	James 1:1-8 ☐	1:9-18 ☐	1:19-27 ☐
84	2:1-13 ☐	2:14-26 ☐	3:1-18 ☐	4:1-10 ☐	4:11-17 ☐	5:1-12 ☐	5:13-20 ☐
85	1 Pet. 1:1-2 ☐	1:3-4 ☐	1:5 ☐	1:6-9 ☐	1:10-12 ☐	1:13-17 ☐	1:18-25 ☐
86	2:1-3 ☐	2:4-8 ☐	2:9-17 ☐	2:18-25 ☐	3:1-13 ☐	3:14-22 ☐	4:1-6 ☐
87	4:7-16 ☐	4:17-19 ☐	5:1-4 ☐	5:5-9 ☐	5:10-14 ☐	2 Pet. 1:1-2 ☐	1:3-4 ☐
88	1:5-8 ☐	1:9-11 ☐	1:12-18 ☐	1:19-21 ☐	2:1-3 ☐	2:4-11 ☐	2:12-22 ☐
89	3:1-6 ☐	3:7-9 ☐	3:10-12 ☐	3:13-15 ☐	3:16 ☐	3:17-18 ☐	1 John 1:1-2 ☐
90	1:3-4 ☐	1:5 ☐	1:6 ☐	1:7 ☐	1:8-10 ☐	2:1-2 ☐	2:3-11 ☐
91	2:12-14 ☐	2:15-19 ☐	2:20-23 ☐	2:24-27 ☐	2:28-29 ☐	3:1-5 ☐	3:6-10 ☐
92	3:11-18 ☐	3:19-24 ☐	4:1-6 ☐	4:7-11 ☐	4:12-15 ☐	4:16—5:3 ☐	5:4-13 ☐
93	5:14-17 ☐	5:18-21 ☐	2 John 1:1-3 ☐	1:4-9 ☐	1:10-13 ☐	3 John 1:1-6 ☐	1:7-14 ☐
94	Jude 1:1-4 ☐	1:5-10 ☐	1:11-19 ☐	1:20-25 ☐	Rev. 1:1-3 ☐	1:4-6 ☐	1:7-11 ☐
95	1:12-13 ☐	1:14-16 ☐	1:17-20 ☐	2:1-6 ☐	2:7 ☐	2:8-9 ☐	2:10-11 ☐
96	2:12-14 ☐	2:15-17 ☐	2:18-23 ☐	2:24-29 ☐	3:1-3 ☐	3:4-6 ☐	3:7-9 ☐
97	3:10-13 ☐	3:14-18 ☐	3:19-22 ☐	4:1-5 ☐	4:6-7 ☐	4:8-11 ☐	5:1-6 ☐
98	5:7-14 ☐	6:1-8 ☐	6:9-17 ☐	7:1-8 ☐	7:9-17 ☐	8:1-6 ☐	8:7-12 ☐
99	8:13—9:11 ☐	9:12-21 ☐	10:1-4 ☐	10:5-11 ☐	11:1-4 ☐	11:5-14 ☐	11:15-19 ☐
100	12:1-4 ☐	12:5-9 ☐	12:10-18 ☐	13:1-10 ☐	13:11-18 ☐	14:1-5 ☐	14:6-12 ☐
101	14:13-20 ☐	15:1-8 ☐	16:1-12 ☐	16:13-21 ☐	17:1-6 ☐	17:7-18 ☐	18:1-8 ☐
102	18:9—19:4 ☐	19:5-10 ☐	19:11-16 ☐	19:17-21 ☐	20:1-6 ☐	20:7-10 ☐	20:11-15 ☐
103	21:1 ☐	21:2 ☐	21:3-8 ☐	21:9-13 ☐	21:14-18 ☐	21:19-21 ☐	21:22-27 ☐
104	22:1 ☐	22:2 ☐	22:3-11 ☐	22:12-15 ☐	22:16-17 ☐	22:18-21 ☐	

Week 5 — Day 1

Today's verses

Luke 15:1-2 Now all the tax collectors and sinners were drawing near to Him to hear Him. And both the Pharisees and the scribes murmured among *themselves*, saying, This man welcomes sinners and eats with them.

John 10:10-11 ...I have come that they may have life and may have *it* abundantly. I am the good Shepherd; the good Shepherd lays down His life for the sheep.

_____
Date

Week 5 — Day 2

Today's verses

Luke 15:4-5 Which man of you, who has a hundred sheep and has lost one of them, does not leave the ninety-nine in the wilderness and go after the one which is lost until he finds it? And when he finds *it*, he lays *it* on his shoulders, rejoicing.

_____
Date

Week 5 — Day 3

Today's verses

Matt. 9:12 ...When He heard *this*, He said, Those who are strong have no need of a physician, but those who are ill.

John 4:14 But whoever drinks of the water that I will give him shall by no means thirst forever; but the water that I will give him will become in him a fountain of water springing up into eternal life.

_____
Date

Week 5 — Day 4

Today's verses

John 21:15-16 Then when they had eaten breakfast, Jesus said to Simon Peter, Simon, *son* of John, do you love Me more than these? He said to Him, Yes, Lord, You know that I love You. He said to him, Feed My lambs. He said to him again a second time, Simon, *son* of John, do you love Me? He said to Him, Yes, Lord, You know that I love You. He said to him, Shepherd My sheep.

_____
Date

Week 5 — Day 5

Today's verses

Acts 20:28 Take heed to yourselves and to all the flock, among whom the Holy Spirit has placed you as overseers to shepherd the church of God...

2 Cor. 3:2-3 You are our letter, inscribed in our hearts, known and read by all men, since you are being manifested that you are a letter of Christ ministered by us, inscribed not with ink but with the Spirit of the living God...

_____
Date

Week 5 — Day 6

Today's verses

2 Cor. 12:15 But I, I will most gladly spend and be utterly spent on behalf of your souls. If I love you more abundantly, am I loved less?

Phil. 2:17 But even if I am being poured out as a drink offering upon the sacrifice and service of your faith, I rejoice, and I rejoice together with you all.

_____
Date

Week 6 — Day 6   Today's verses

2 Cor. 13:14 The grace of the Lord Jesus Christ and the love of God and the fellowship of the Holy Spirit be with you all.

John 6:63 It is the Spirit who gives life; the flesh profits nothing; the words which I have spoken to you are spirit and are life.

_____
Date

Week 6 — Day 5   Today's verses

Exo. 3:18 …And you shall come, you and the elders of Israel, to the king of Egypt, and you shall say to him, Jehovah, the God of the Hebrews, has met with us; and now let us go a three days' journey into the wilderness that we may sacrifice to Jehovah our God.

2 Cor. 11:2 For I am jealous over you with a jealousy of God; for I betrothed you to one husband to present *you as* a pure virgin to Christ.

_____
Date

Week 6 — Day 4   Today's verses

1 Thes. 2:12 So that you might walk in a manner worthy of God, who calls you into His own kingdom and glory.

Phil. 1:21 For to me, to live is Christ…

_____
Date

Week 6 — Day 3   Today's verses

Col. 3:10-11 And have put on the new man, which is being renewed unto full knowledge according to the image of Him who created him, where there cannot be Greek and Jew, circumcision and uncircumcision, barbarian, Scythian, slave, free man, but Christ is all and in all.

_____
Date

Week 6 — Day 2   Today's verses

John 15:4 Abide in Me and I in you. As the branch cannot bear fruit of itself unless it abides in the vine, so neither can you unless you abide in Me.

6:57 As the living Father has sent Me and I live because of the Father, so he who eats Me, he also shall live because of Me.

_____
Date

Week 6 — Day 1   Today's verses

John 21:16 He said to him again a second time, Simon, *son* of John, do you love Me? He said to Him, Yes, Lord, You know that I love You. He said to him, Shepherd My sheep.

1 Pet. 5:2 Shepherd the flock of God among you, overseeing not under compulsion but willingly, according to God; not by seeking gain through base means but eagerly.

_____
Date